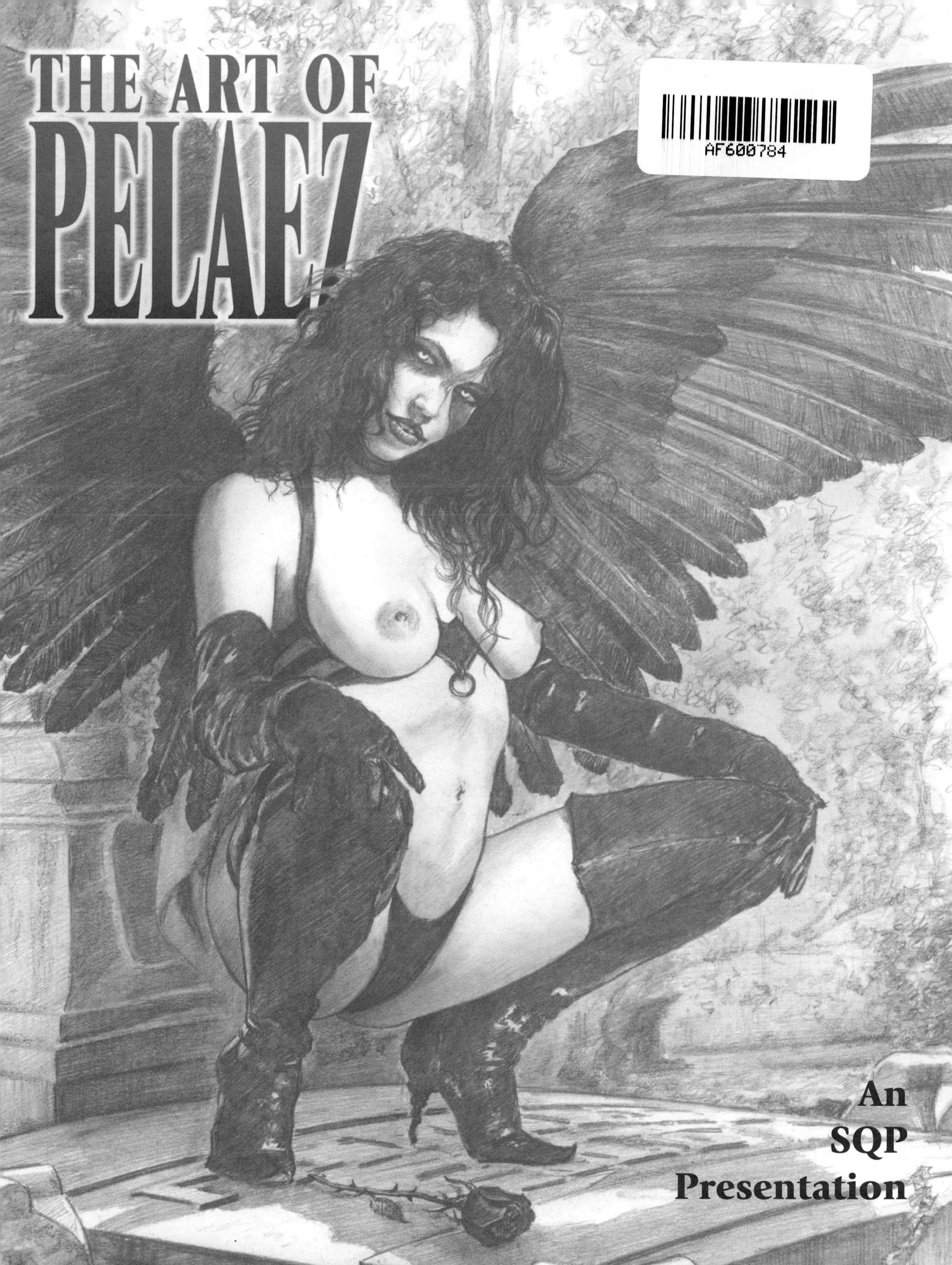
THE ART OF
PELAEZ
An
SQP
Presentation

PELAEZ "PICTURE PERFECT"

Joan Pelaez is a man of unique talents, as he can make the ordinary seem quite fantastic, and the fantastic seem extraordinary possible. And then there's his ability to illustrate women - that's something approaching the truly inspired! From the first time he presented a drawing for a Gallery Girls collection, we knew we had a fan-fave in the making! This book will provide ample evidence to Senor Pelaez' charms!

A native of Spain, he was born in 1957, in Premià de Mar in Barcelona. At an early age, he discovered his passion for drawing. By the time he was 14 he had showed so much drive and talent he became an apprentice at a studio that showcased some of the greatest commercial artists of the time, including Carlos Giménez, Joaquin Blázquez, and Adolfo Usero. While picking up real-world experience and learning from true masters, he also took the time to receive more formal training at the prestigious Real Circulo Artistico de Barcelona.

After this education, he joined local studios and collaborated with other artists and writers on projects, making a reputation for himself as a solid illustrator and painter. It was when he created the artwork for the book " El color de la Nada" (The Color of Anything) by the author Jose Luis Navas that he caught a very lucky break. The book was making a splashy presentation at the Hotel Princesa Sofía in Barcelona, which allowed Pelaez to showcase his work. After this exhibition he came in contact with a variety of art agencies, including Dalmau Editors, which finally gave him an opening to an international market. Since that time, he's worked for publications like Harlequin, Thyndale, Random House, Heavy Metal and of course, the greatly appreciated pencils and paintings for SQP.

Pelaez has also worked with cinema and video production companies like Filmax, Motion Pictures, Lauren Films, CB Films,Recorvision, and TeleVideoFilms doing video covers and film posters, and with advertising and publicity companies such as Bassat, Ogilvy and Mather and the agency Tiempo/BBDO.

Like many other artists today, Pelaez is also fascinated with the process of digitally creating his work. Although we're in love with the low-tech wonder of pencil on paper and paint on board, the possibilities of what Pelaez will accomplish in the future on a virtual canvas has us looking forward to the actual "El color de la Nada"!

Sal Quartuccio & Bob Keenan
Publishers

A special note of thanks to Esteve and Jose Dalmau for all their help in the creation of this book, and for introducing our fans to this amazing artist!

THE ART OF PELAEZ
Volume One

Book design by Grassy Knoll Studios.

Published by
SQP Inc.
PO Box 248 - Columbus, NJ 08022

Sal Quartuccio & Bob Keenan - Publishers

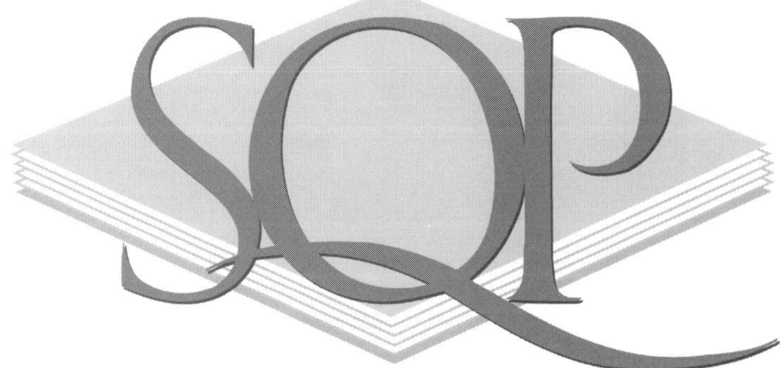

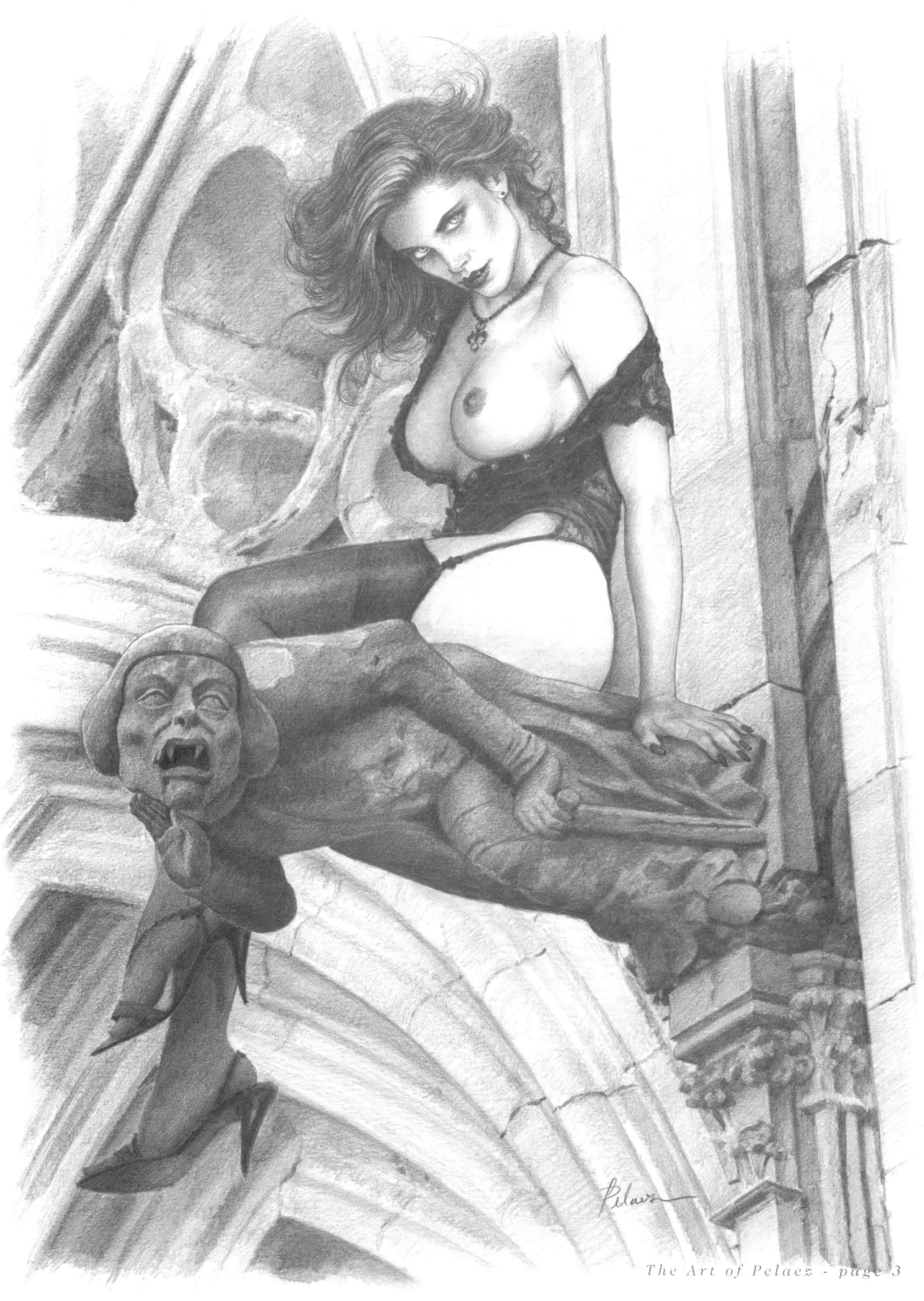

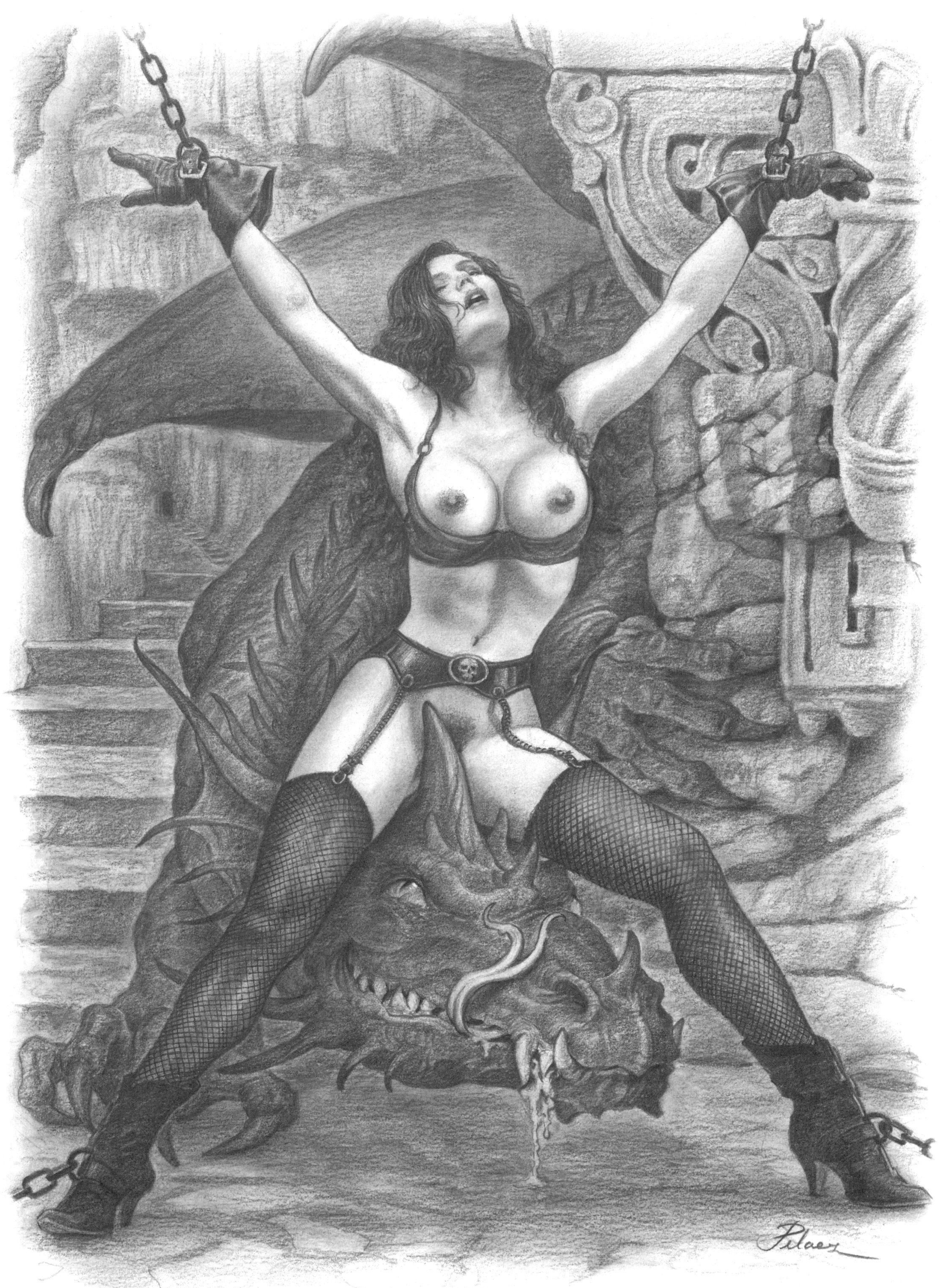
Pelaez

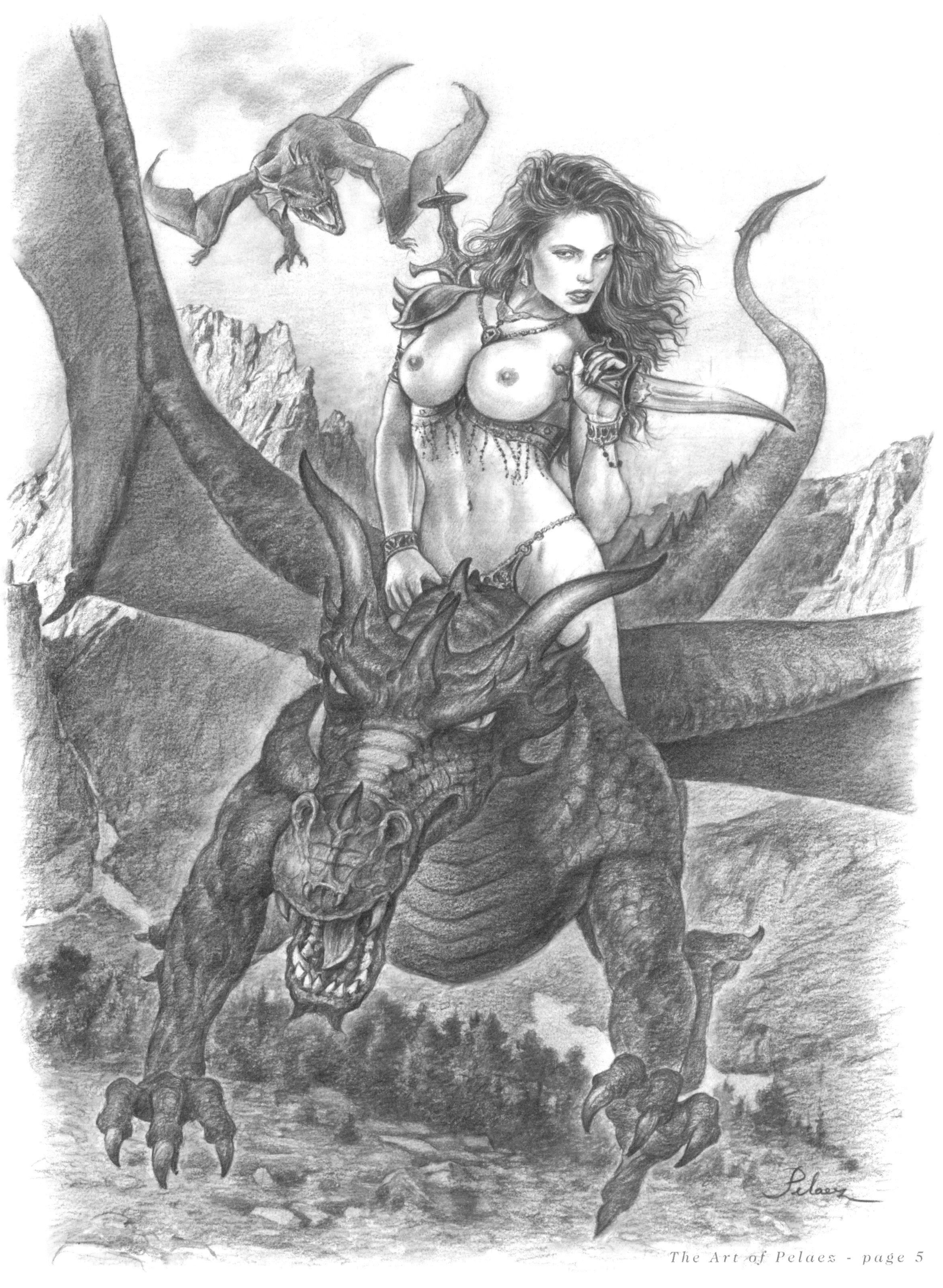
Pelaez

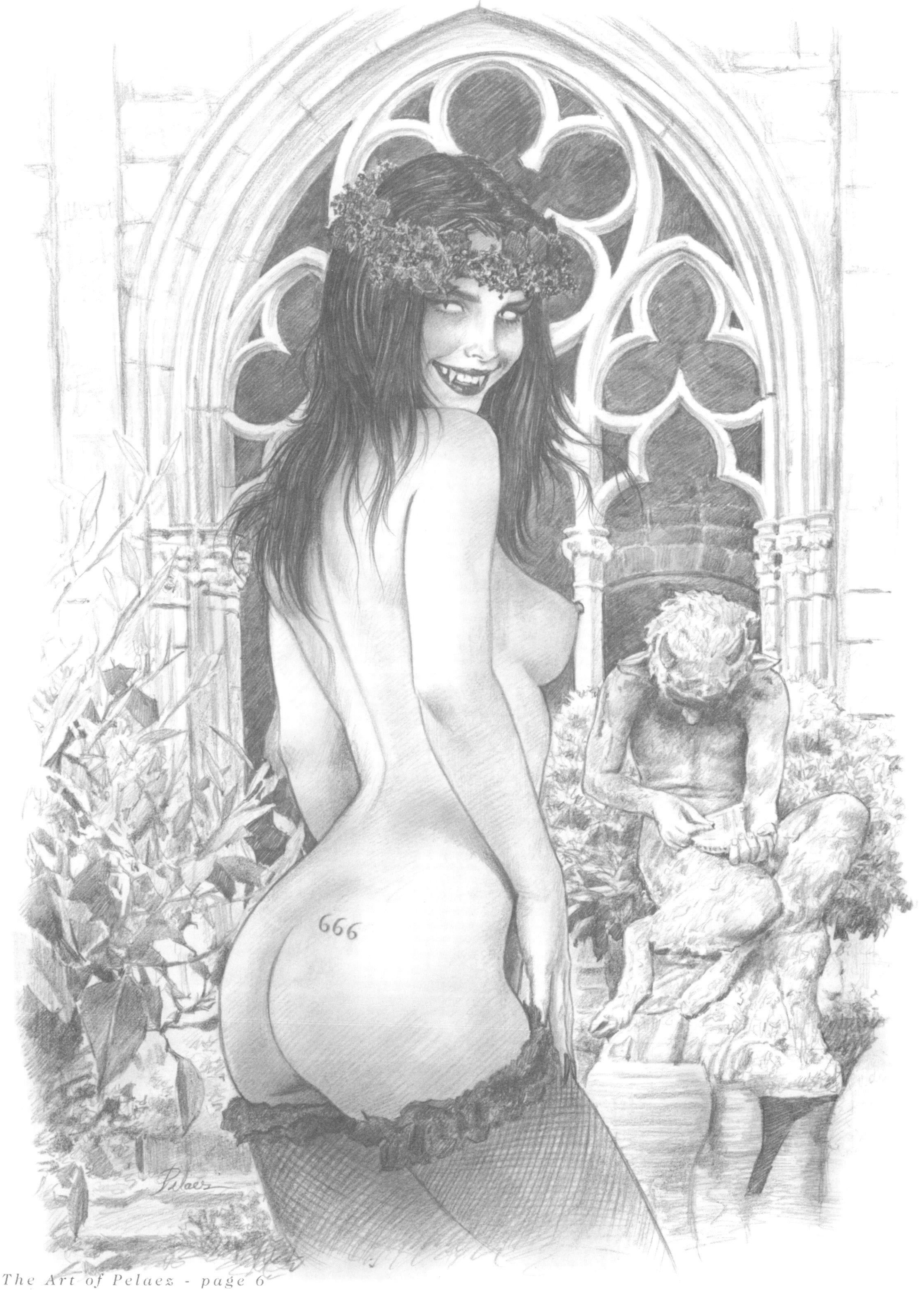
666
Pelaez

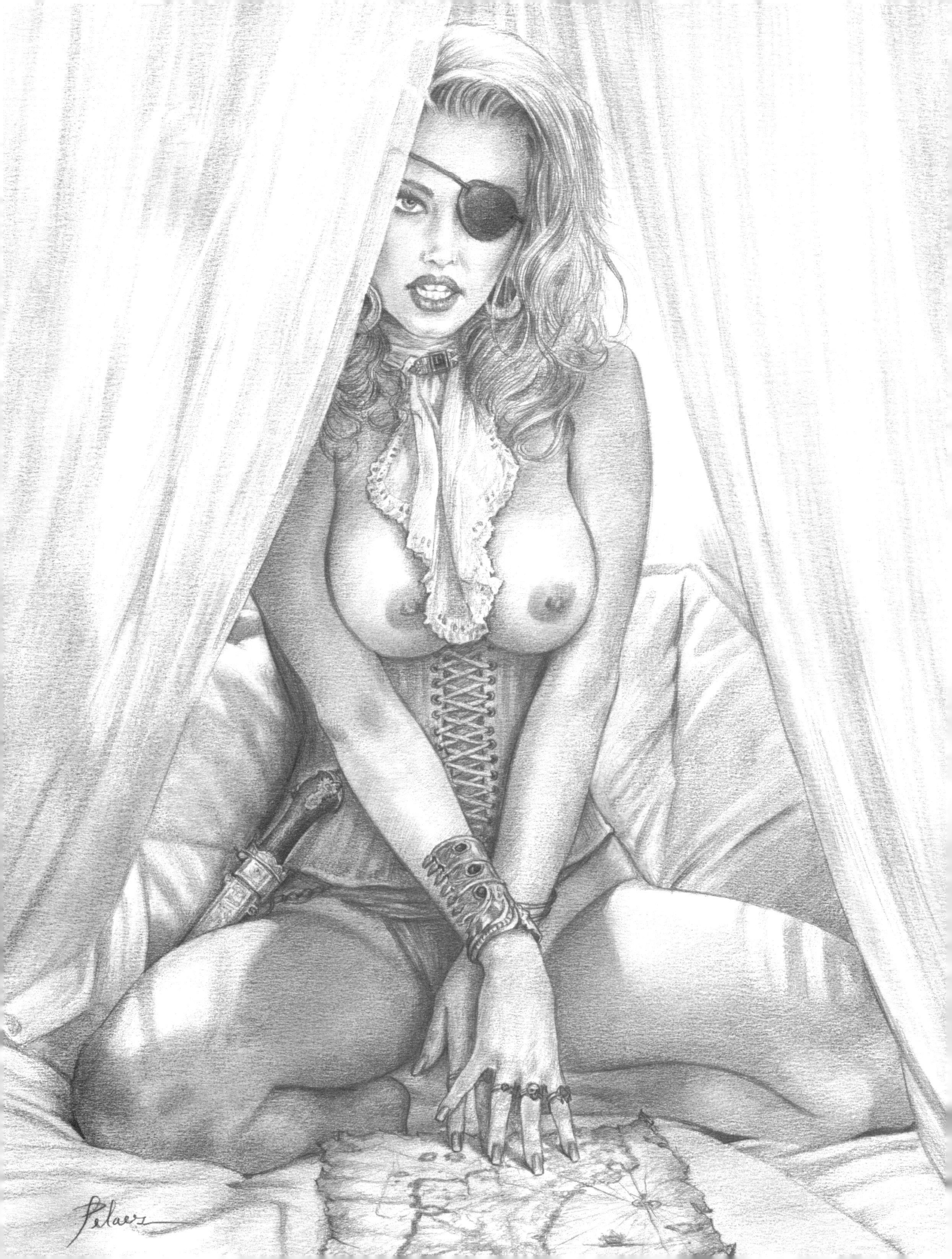
Pelaez

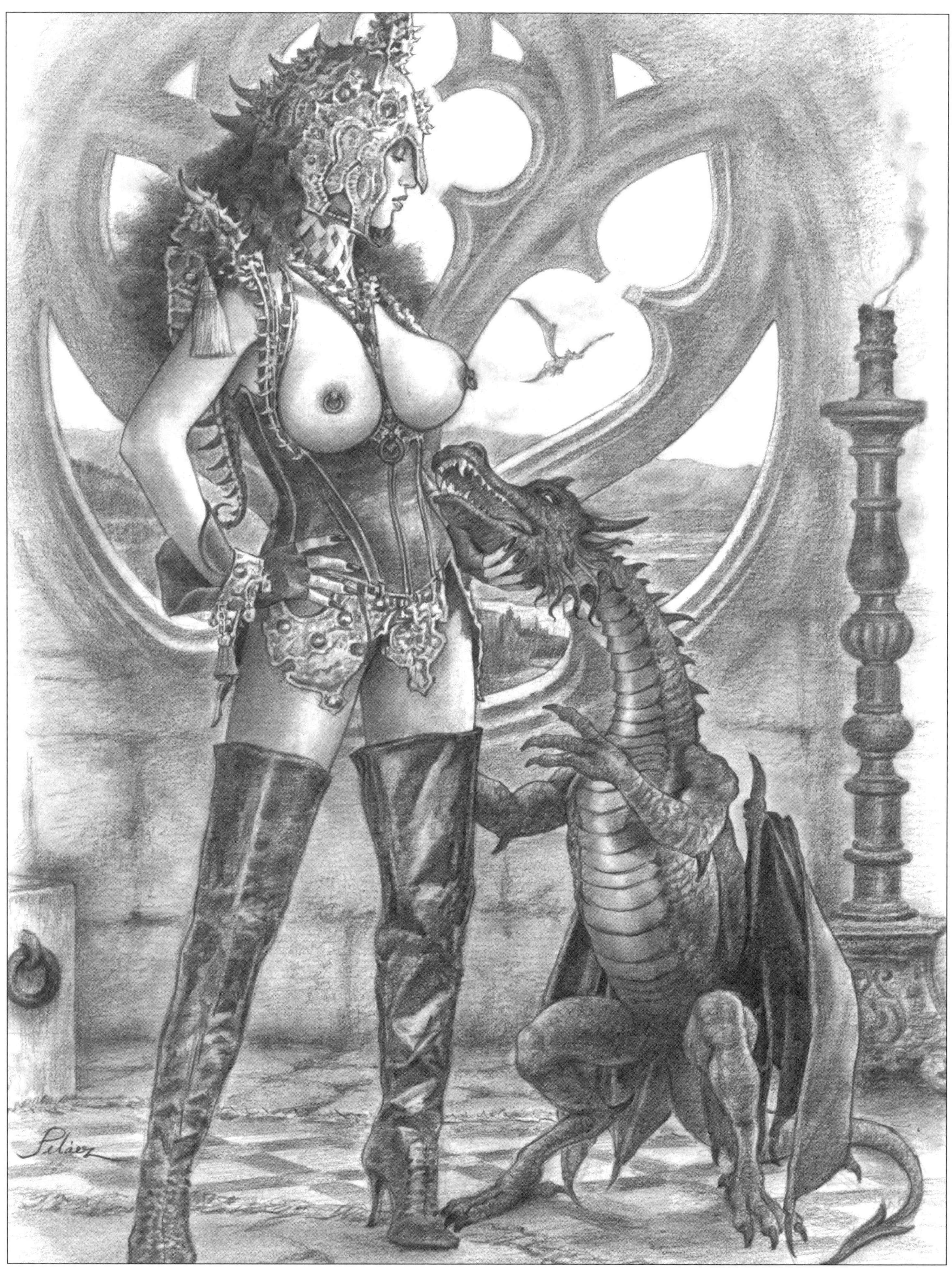
Peláez

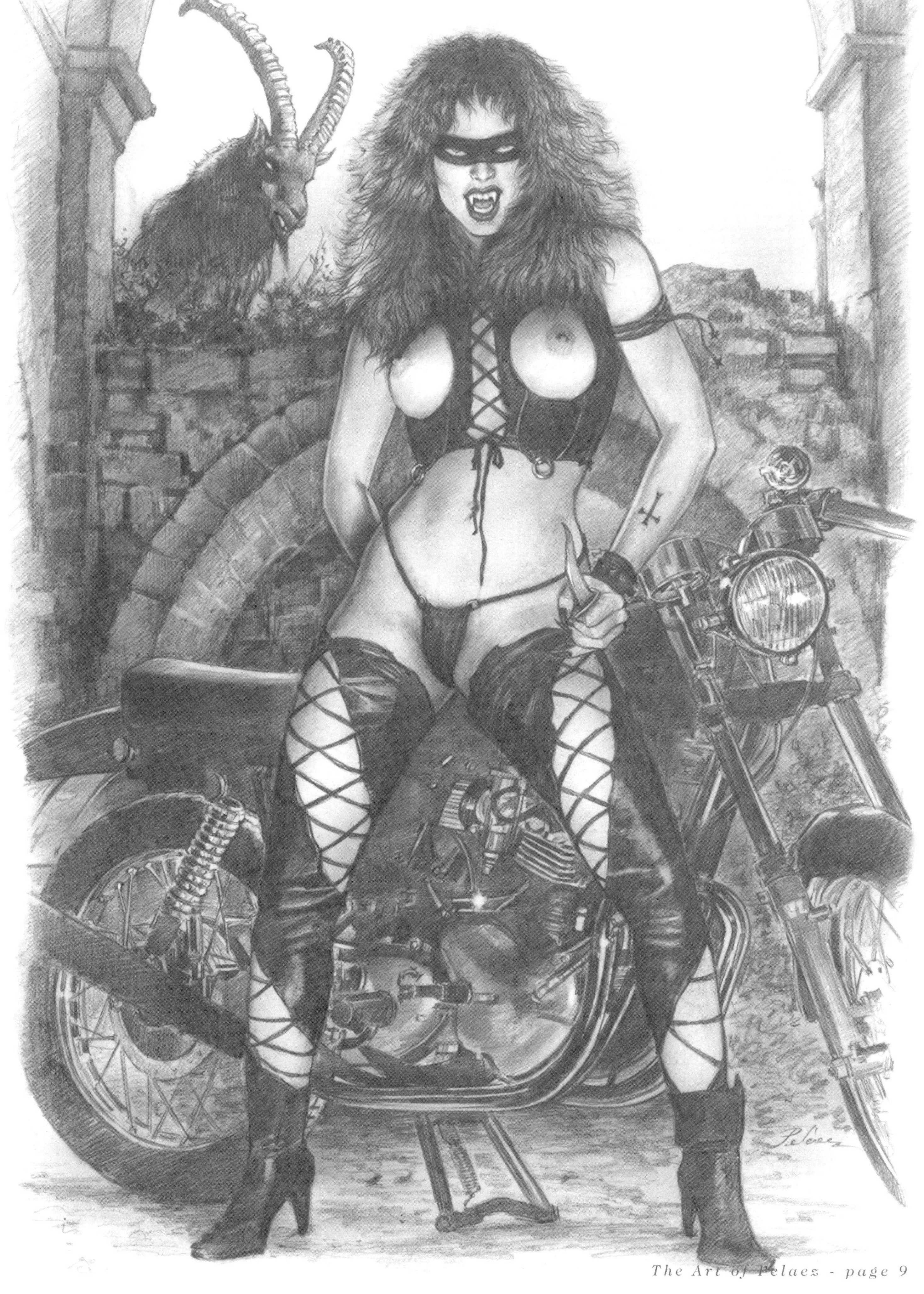
Pelaez

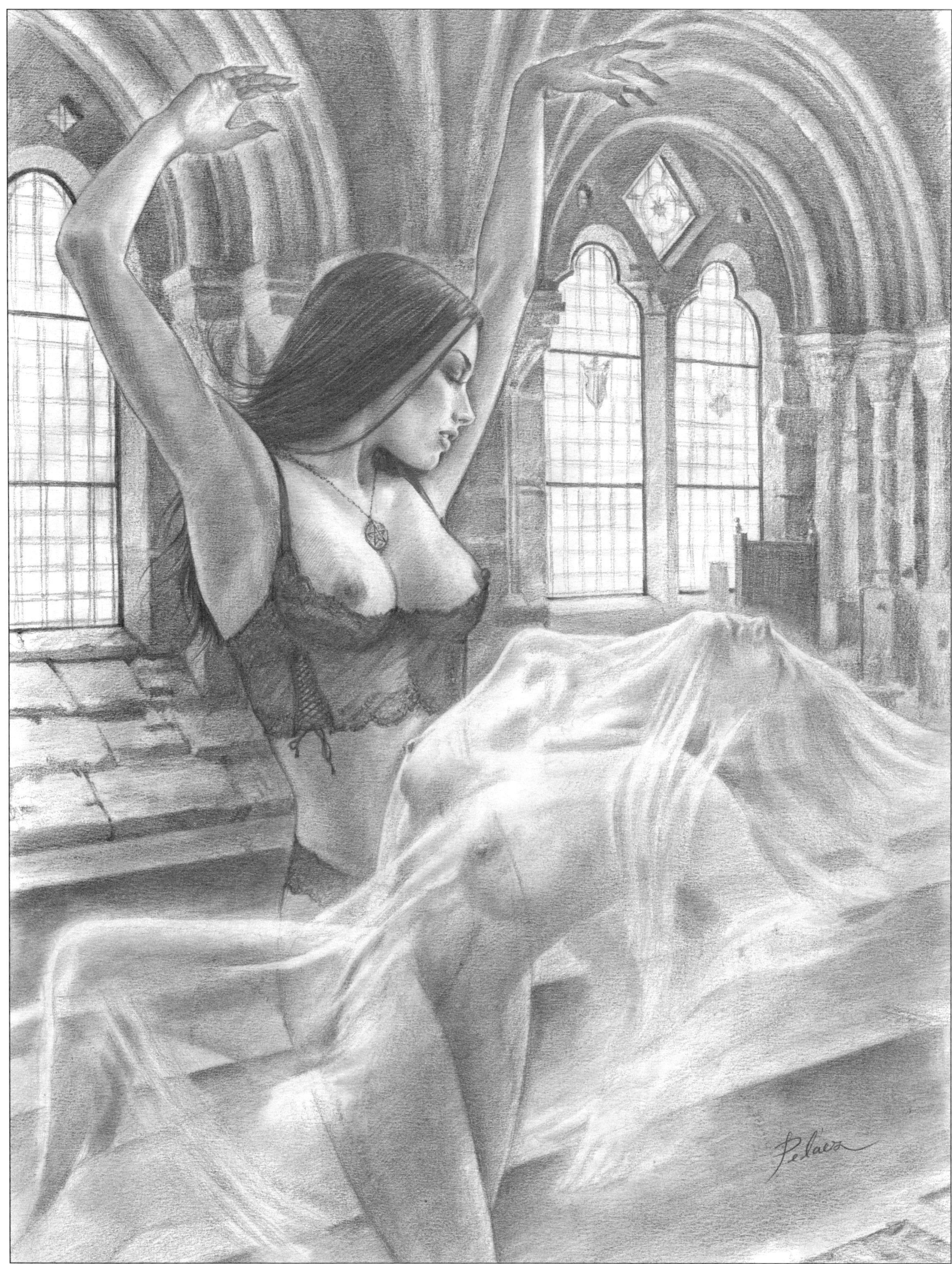
Pelaez

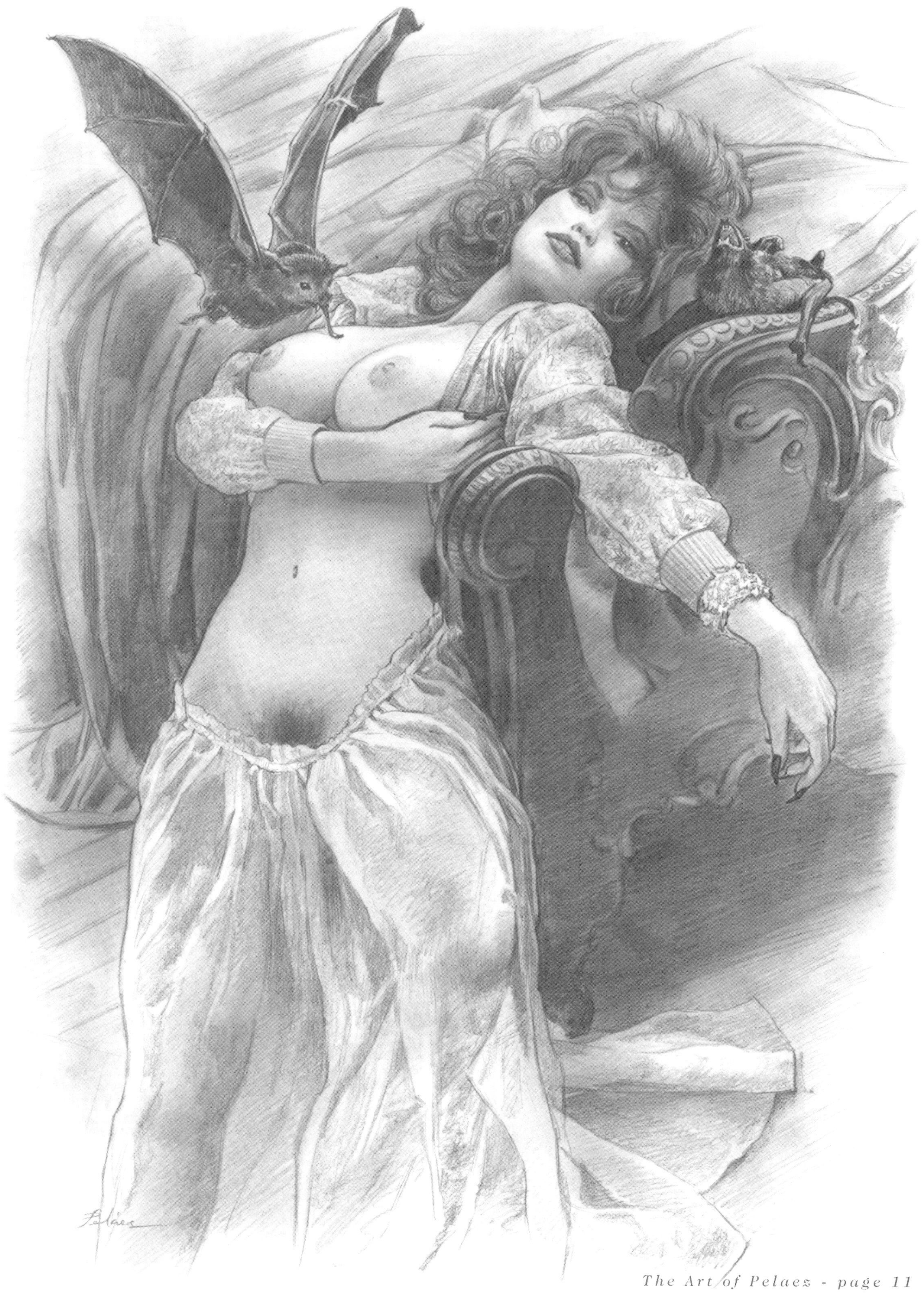

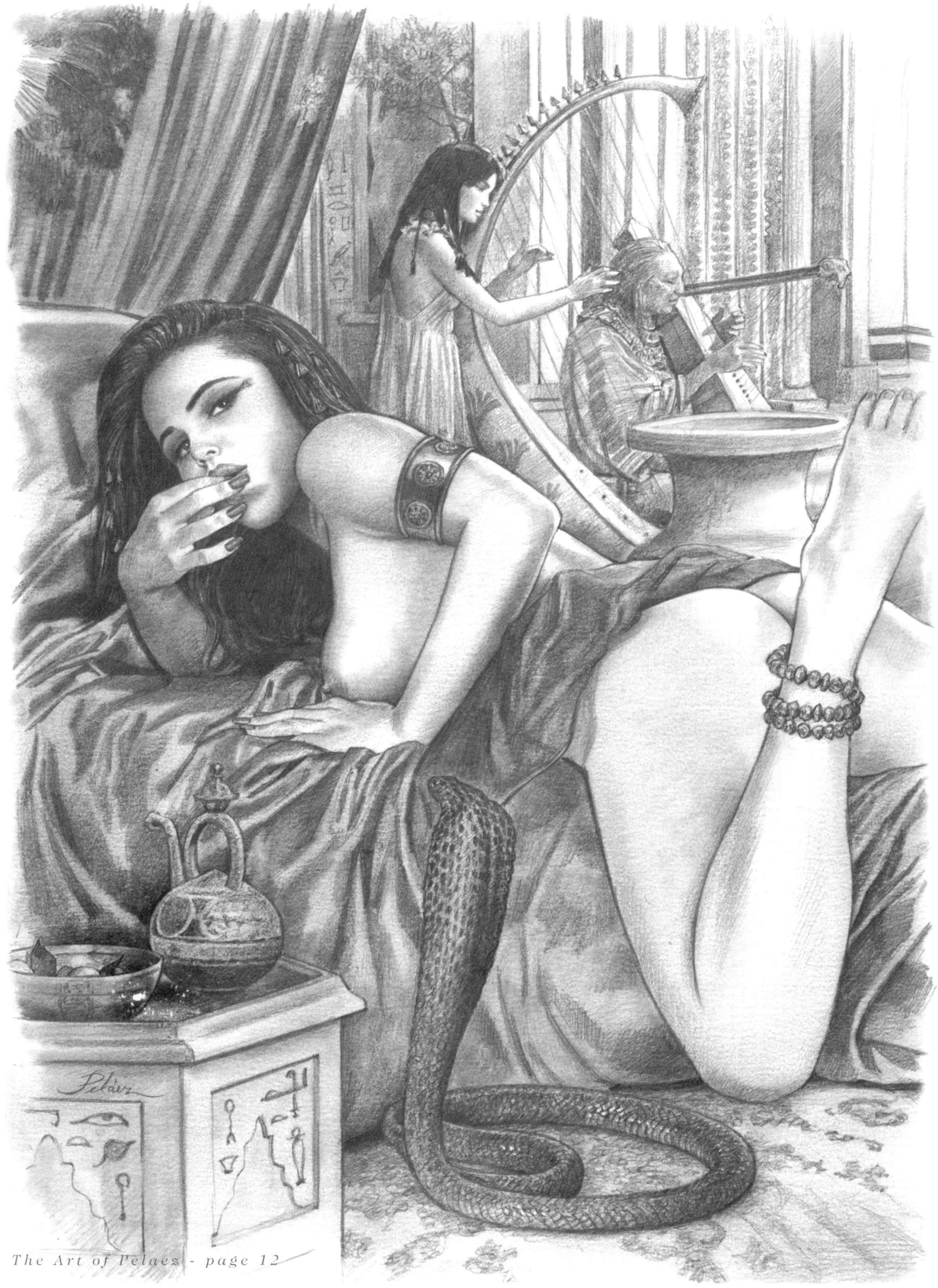

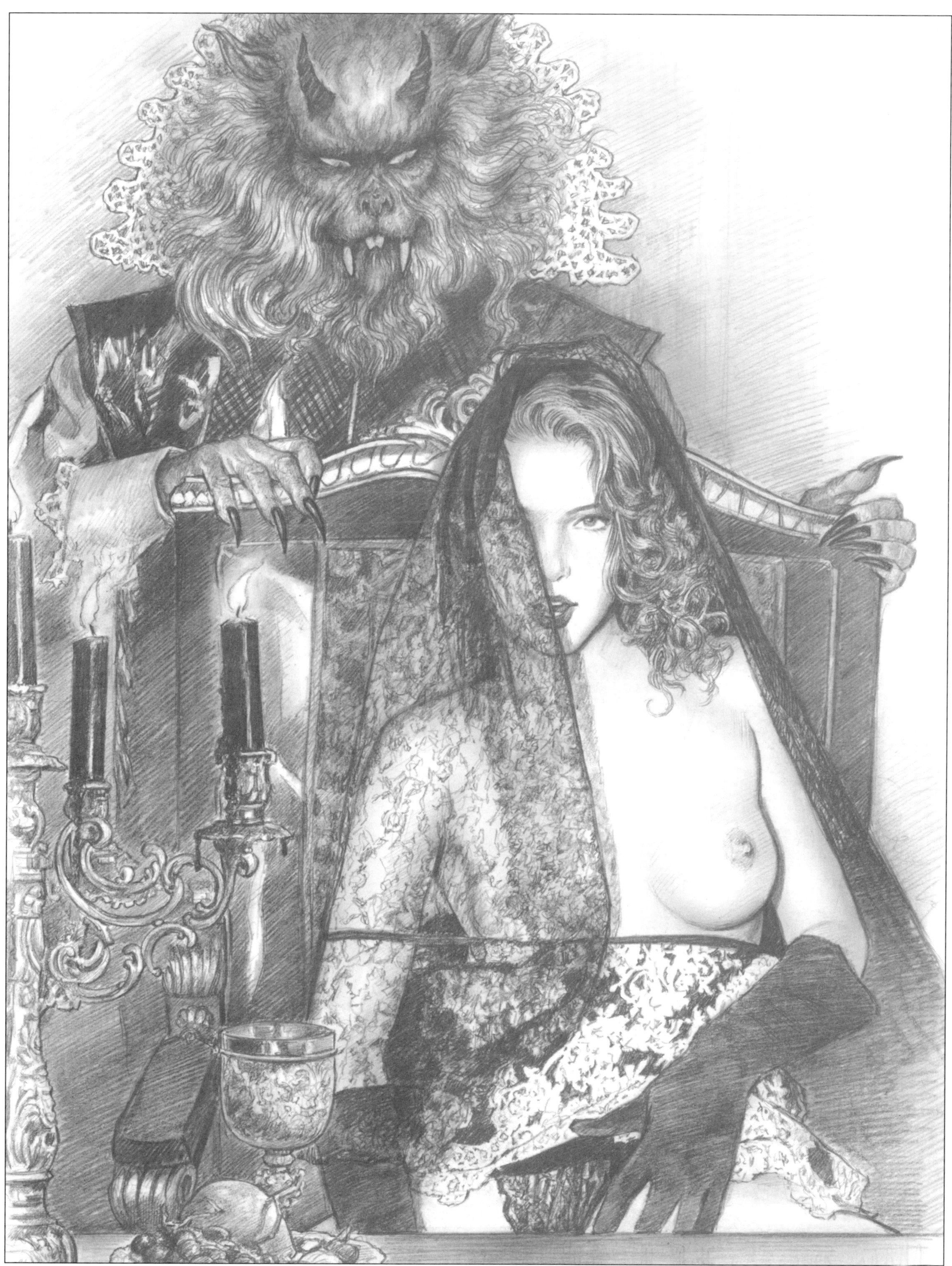

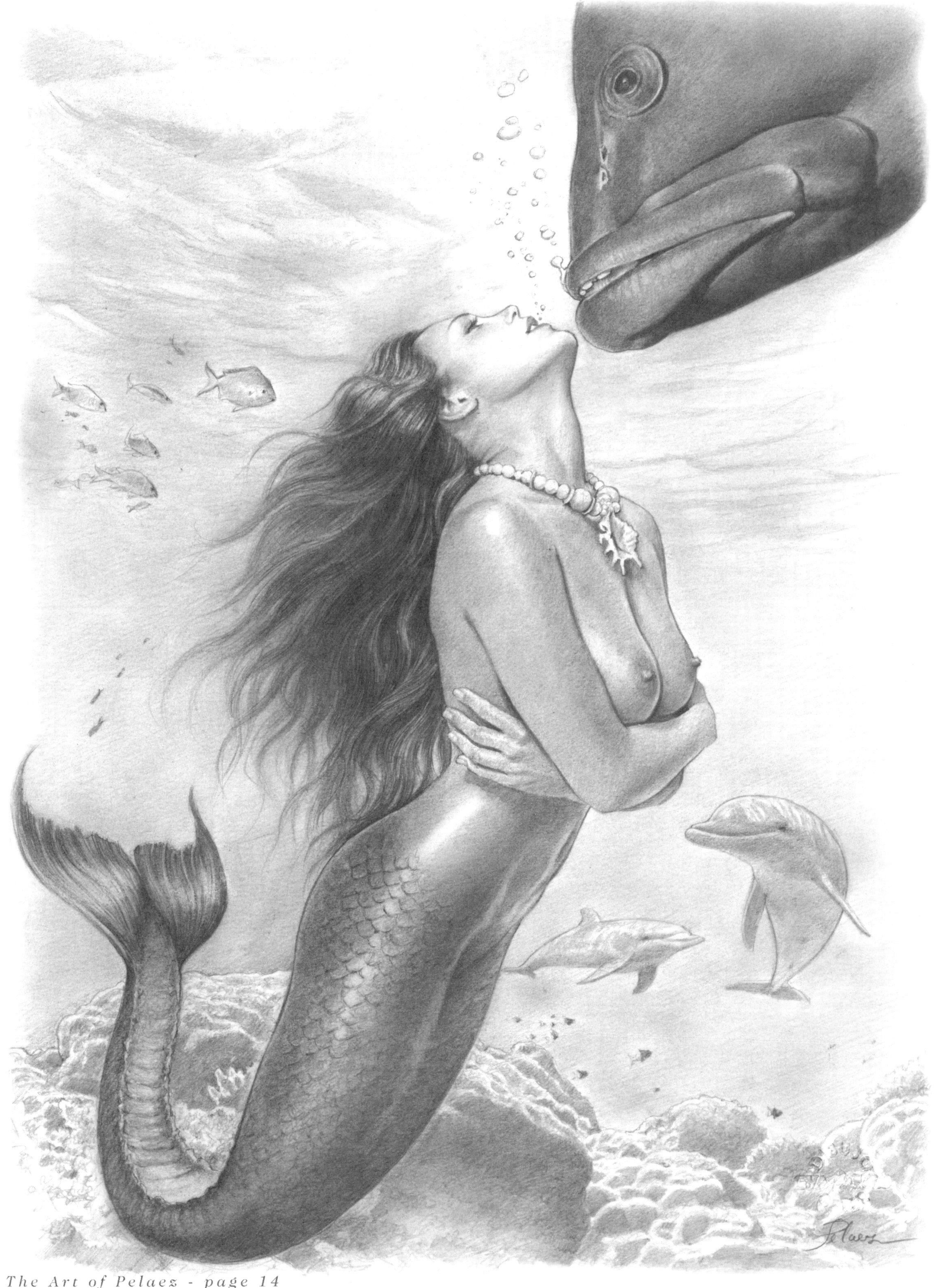
Pelaez

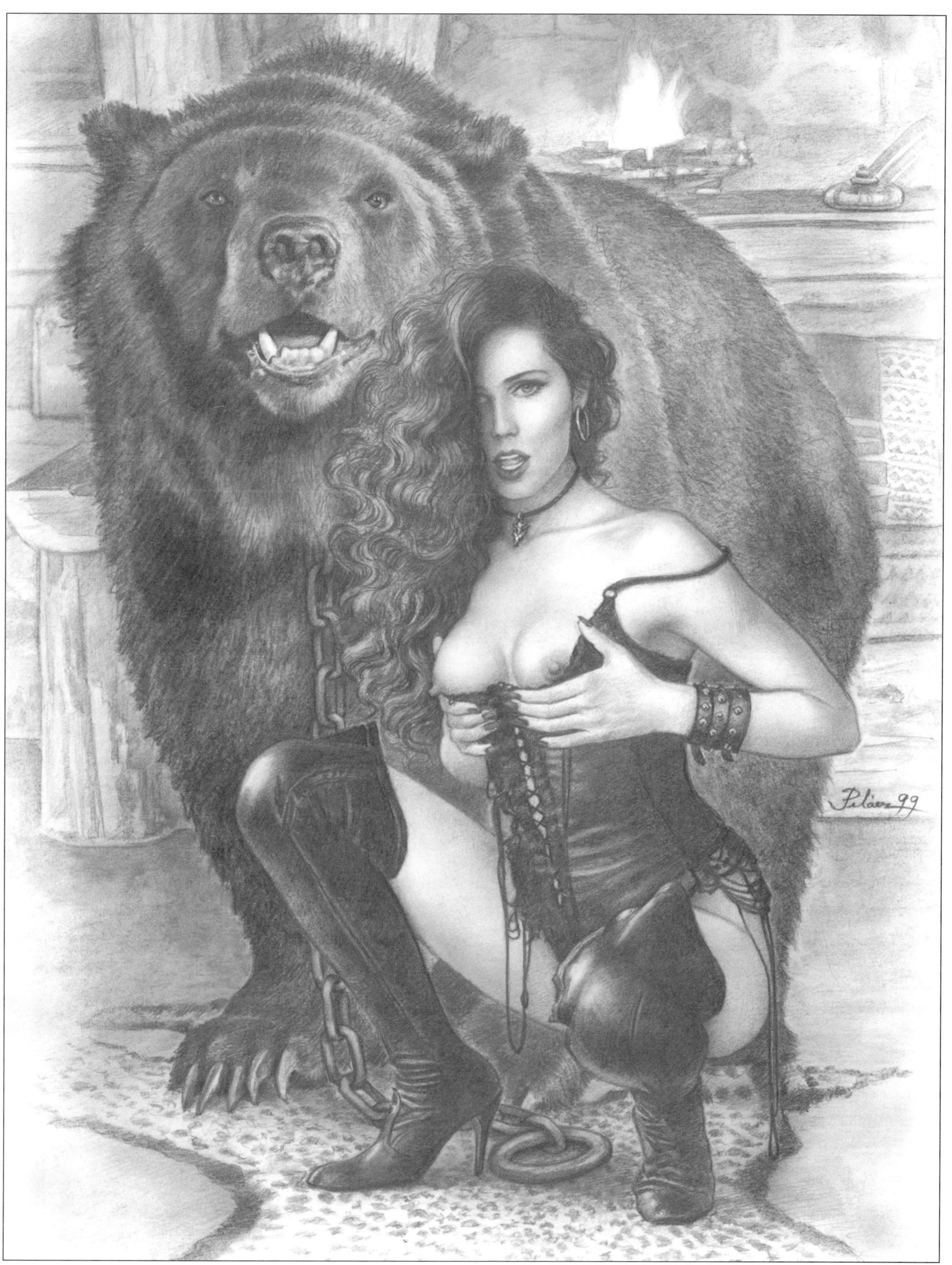
Peláez 99

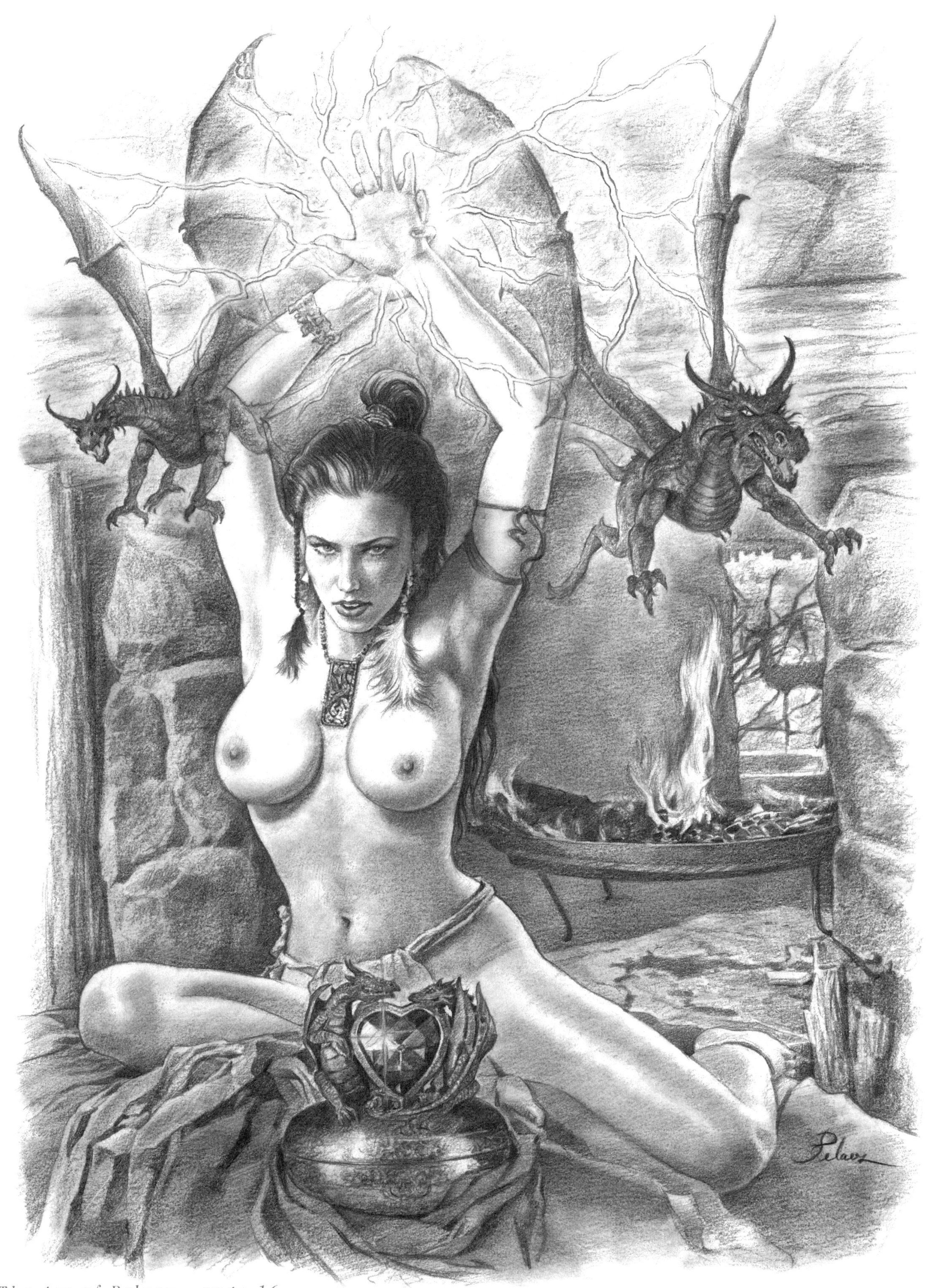
Pelaez

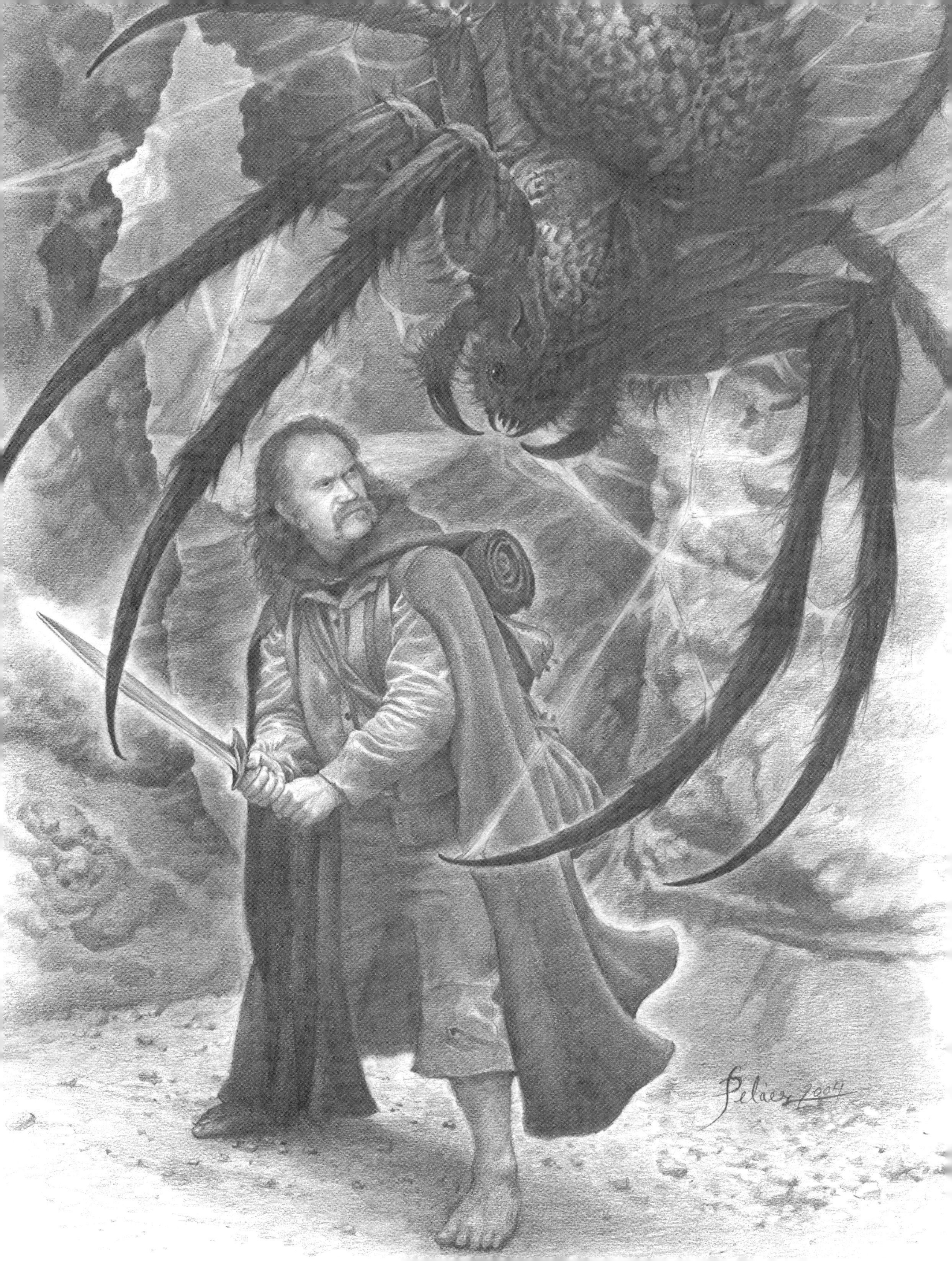

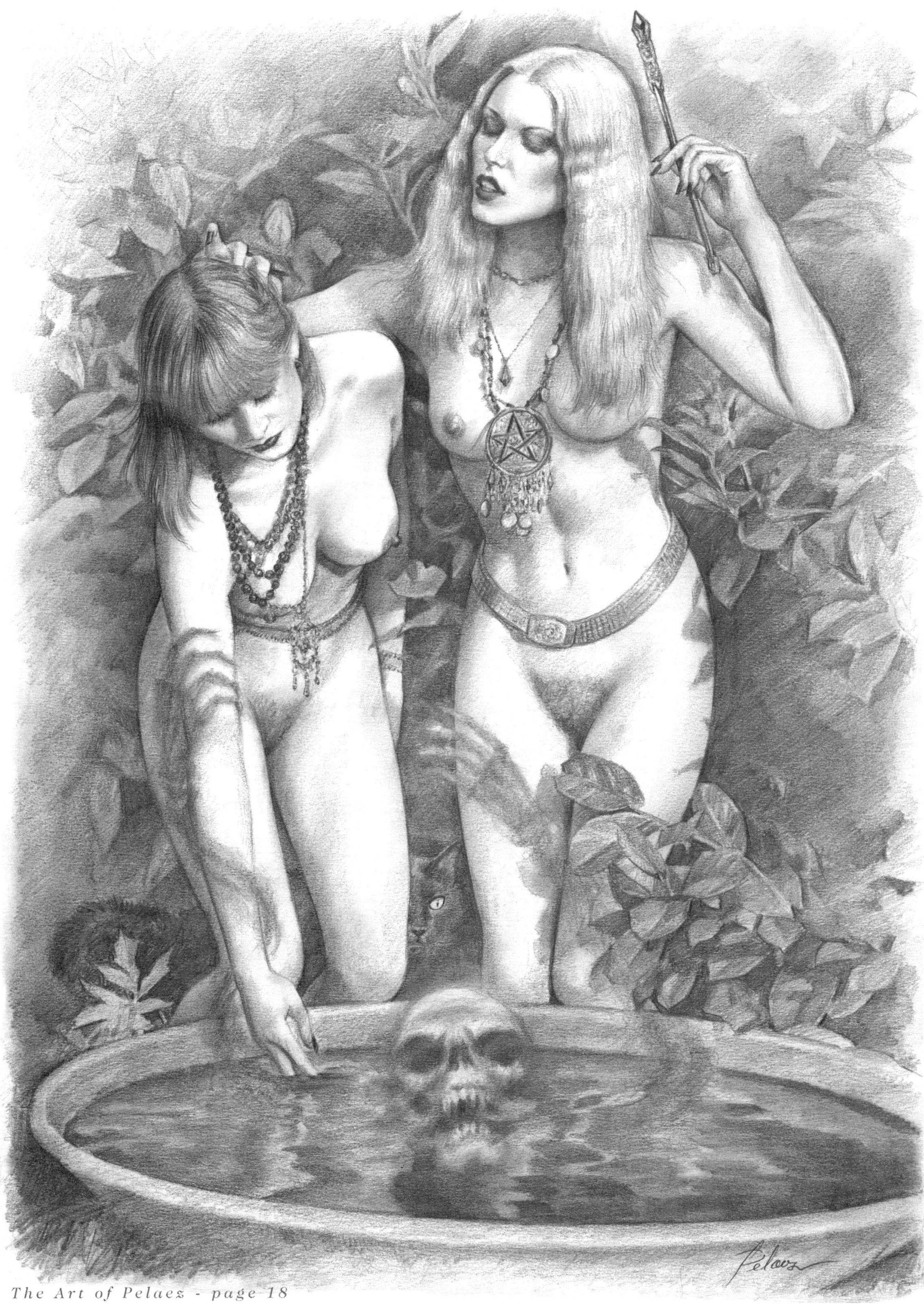
Pelaez

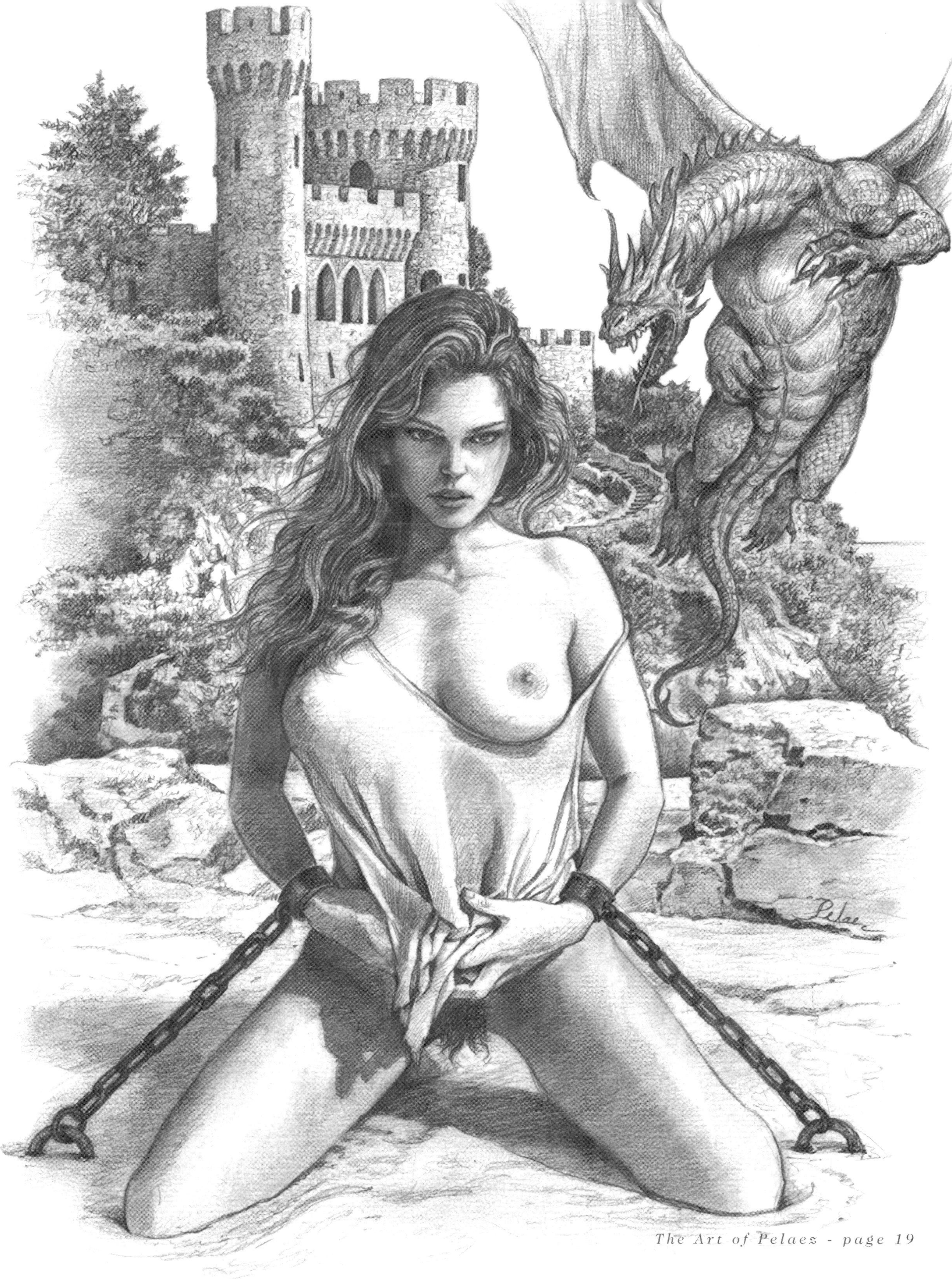
Pelaez

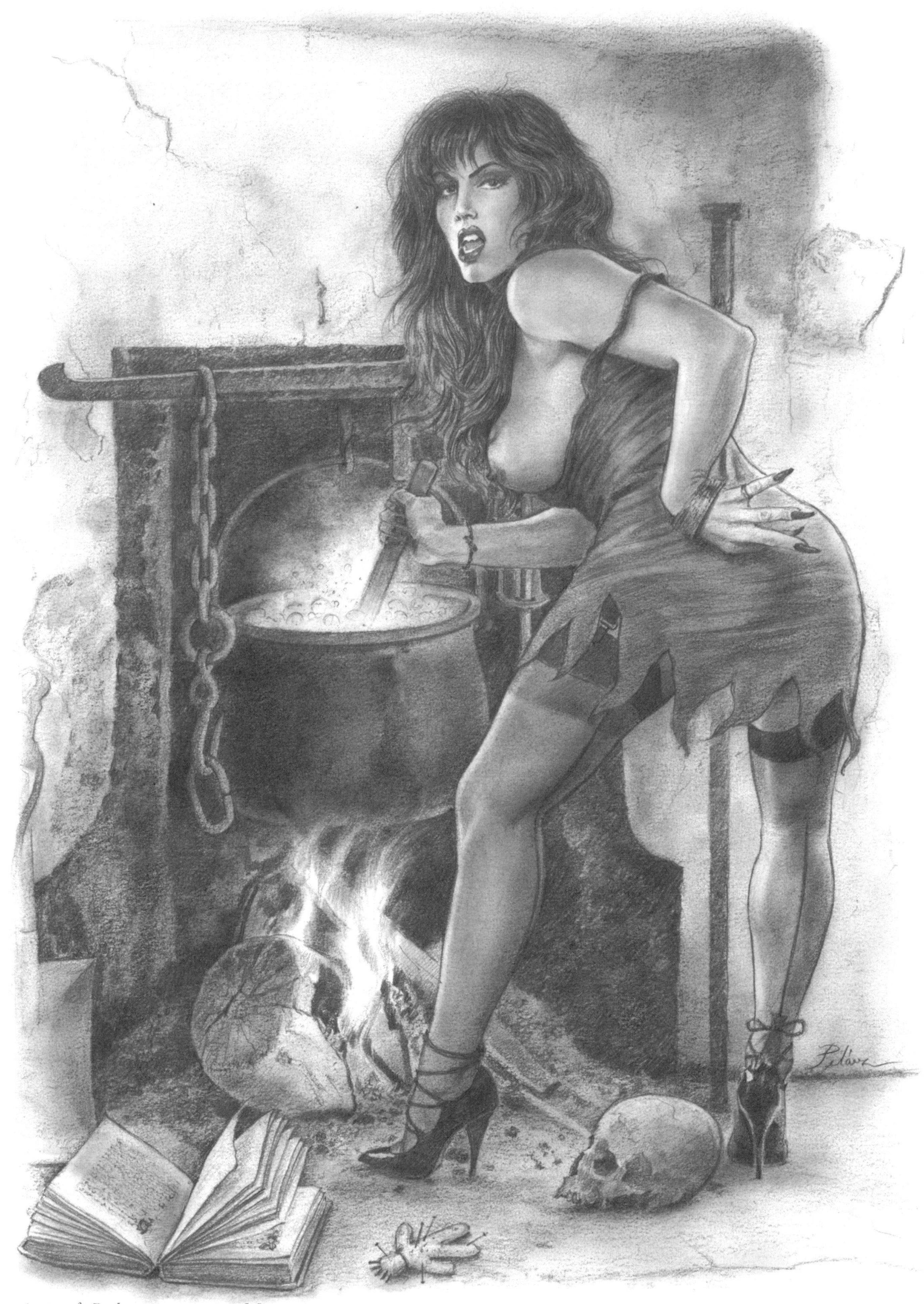

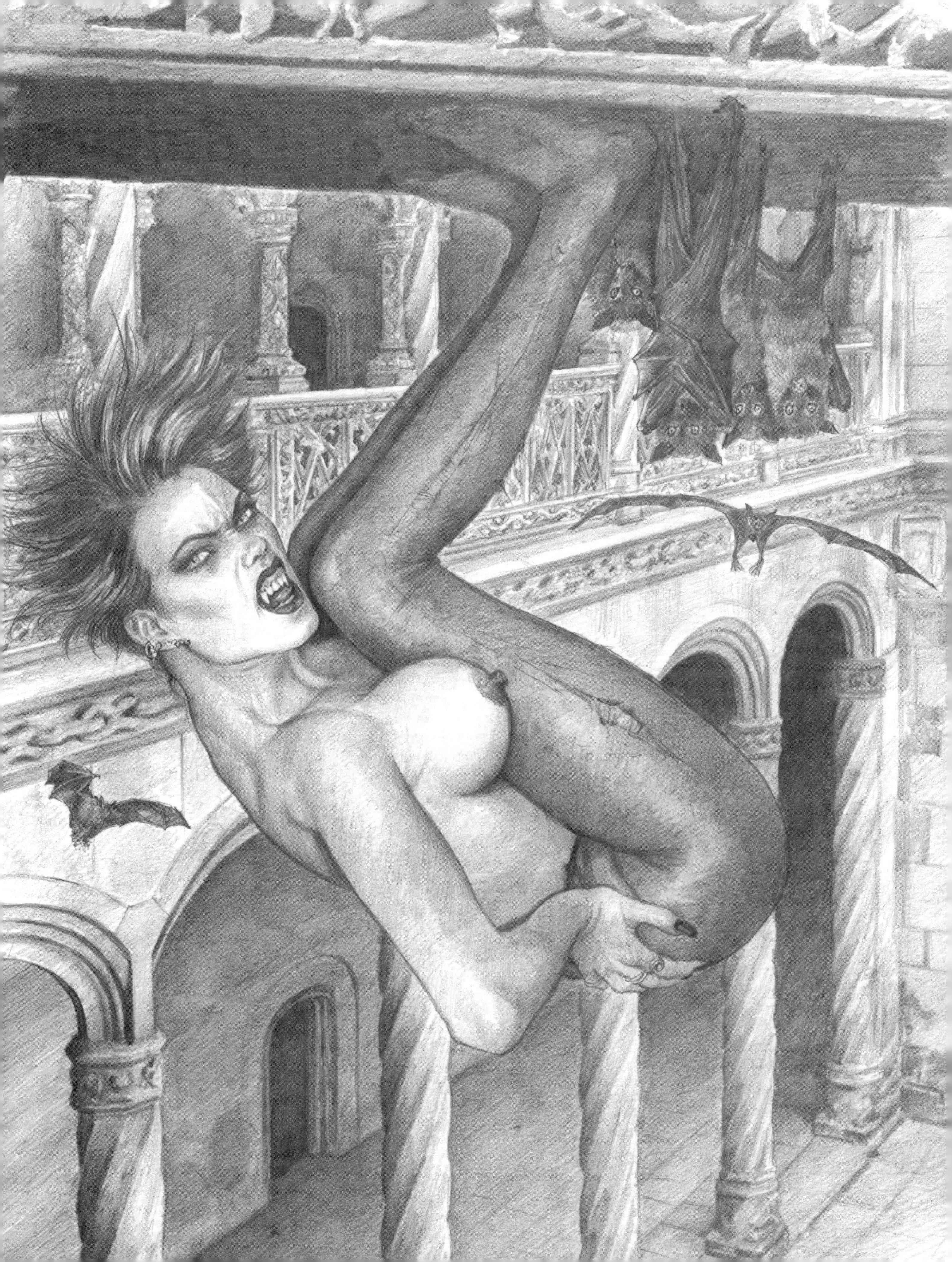

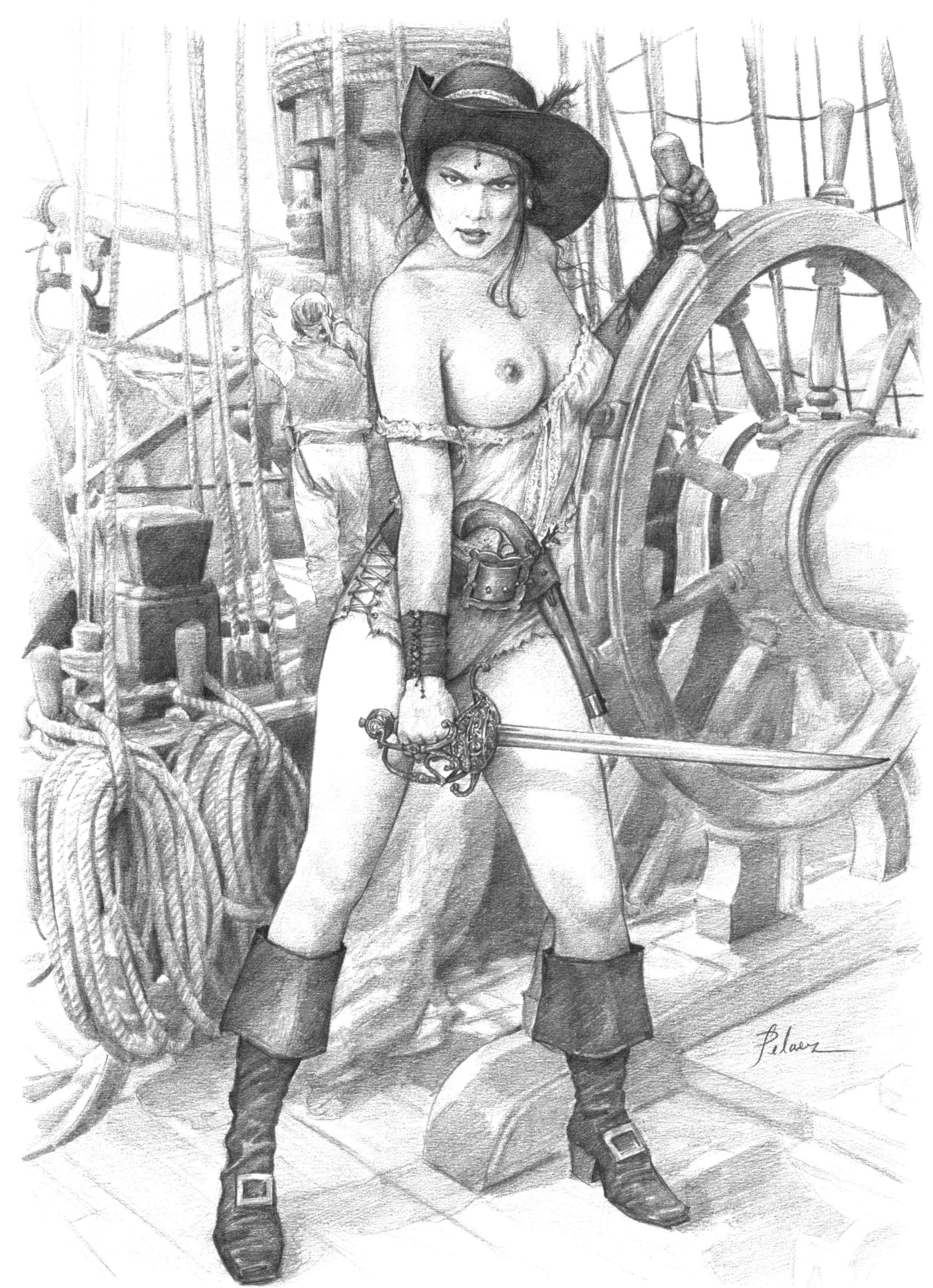
Pelaez

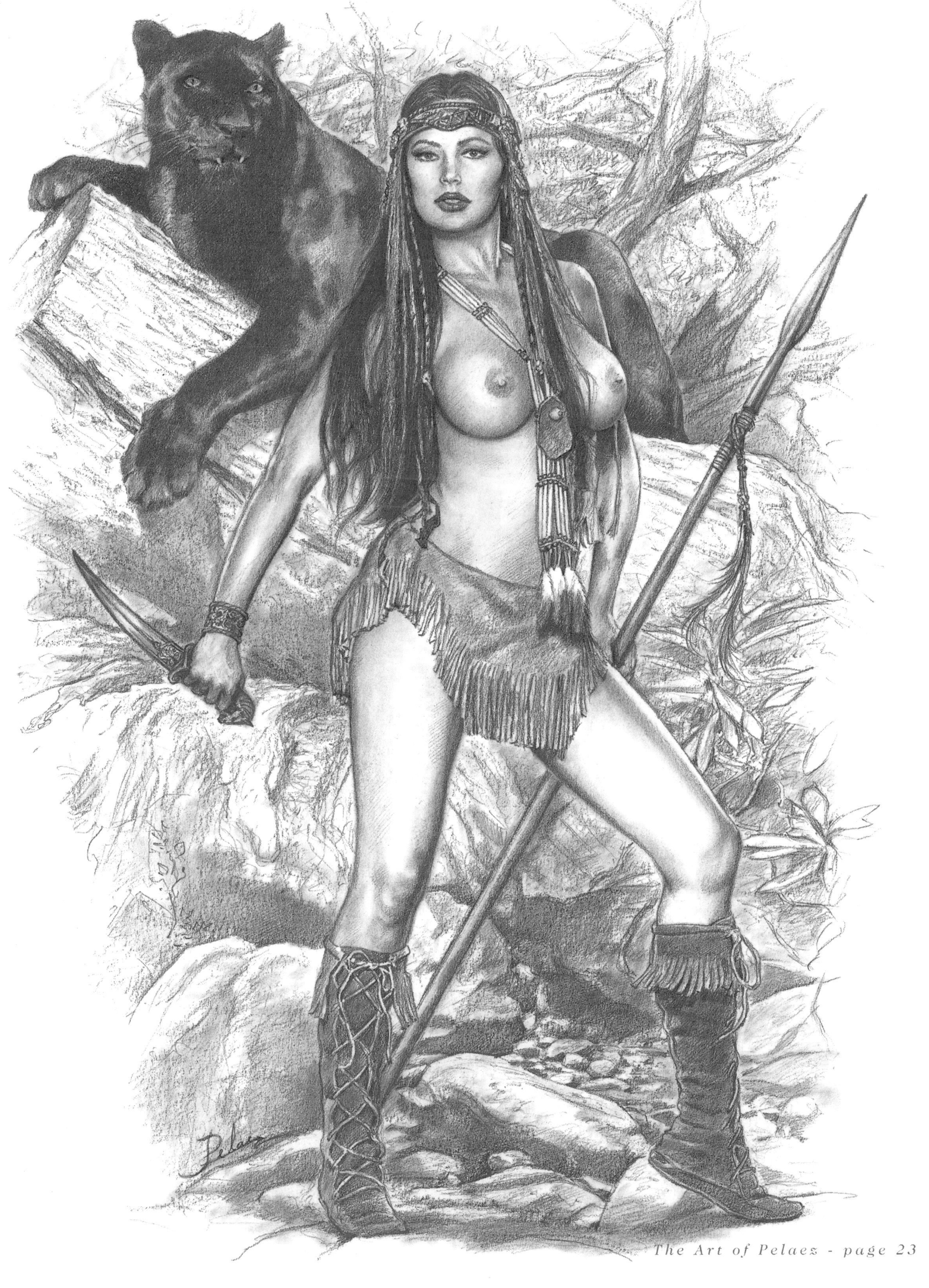
Pelaez

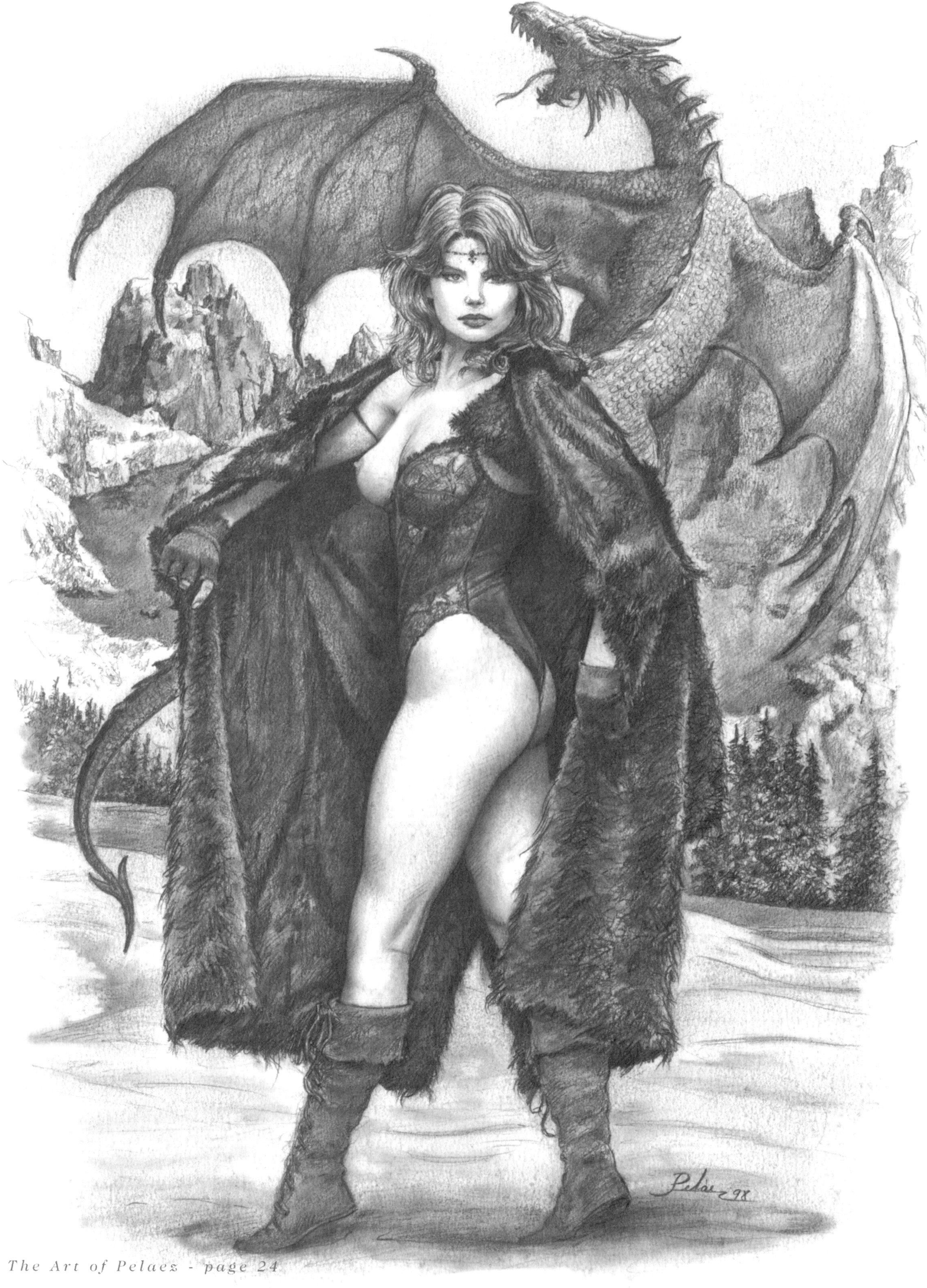
Pelaez 98

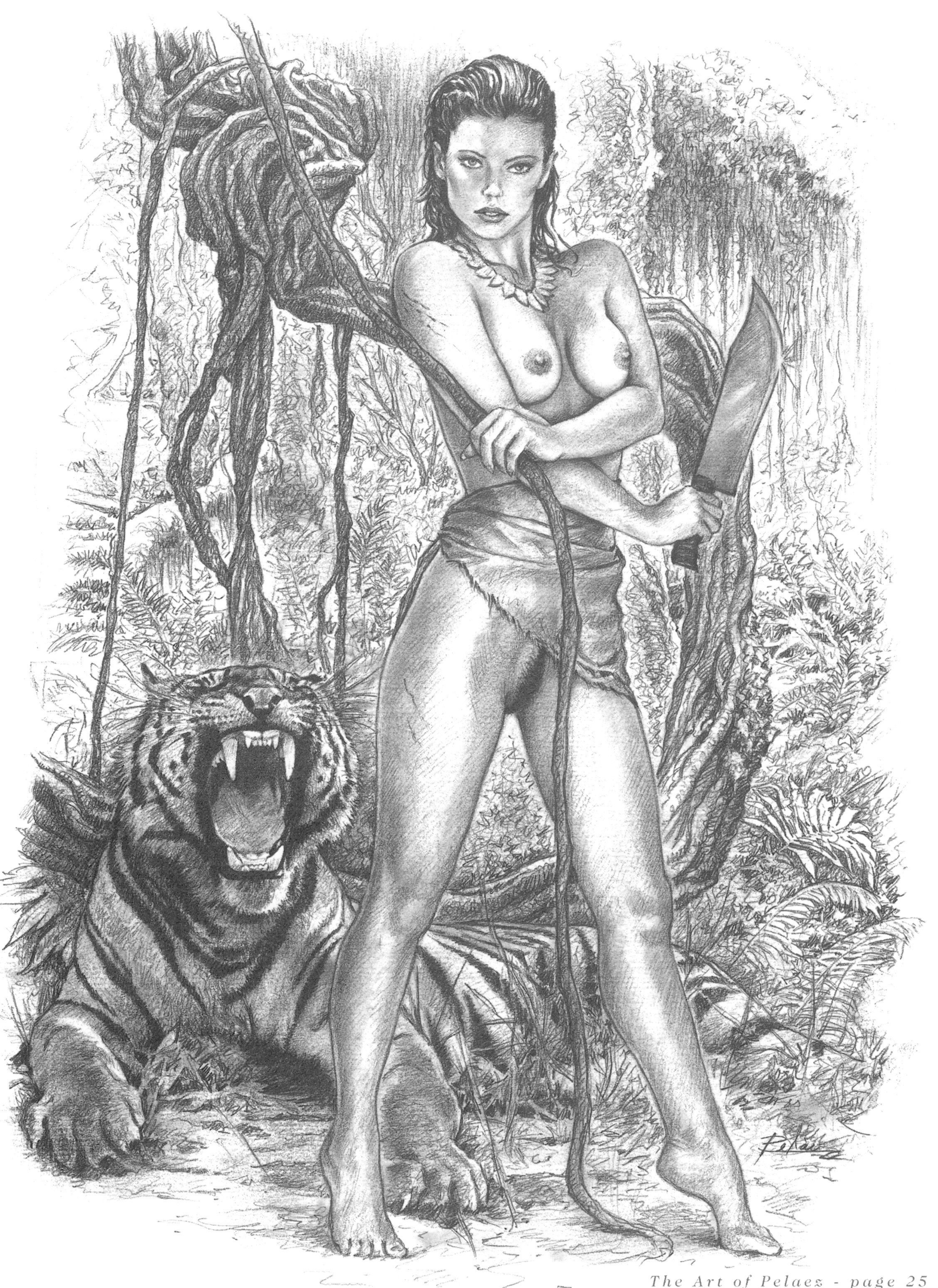

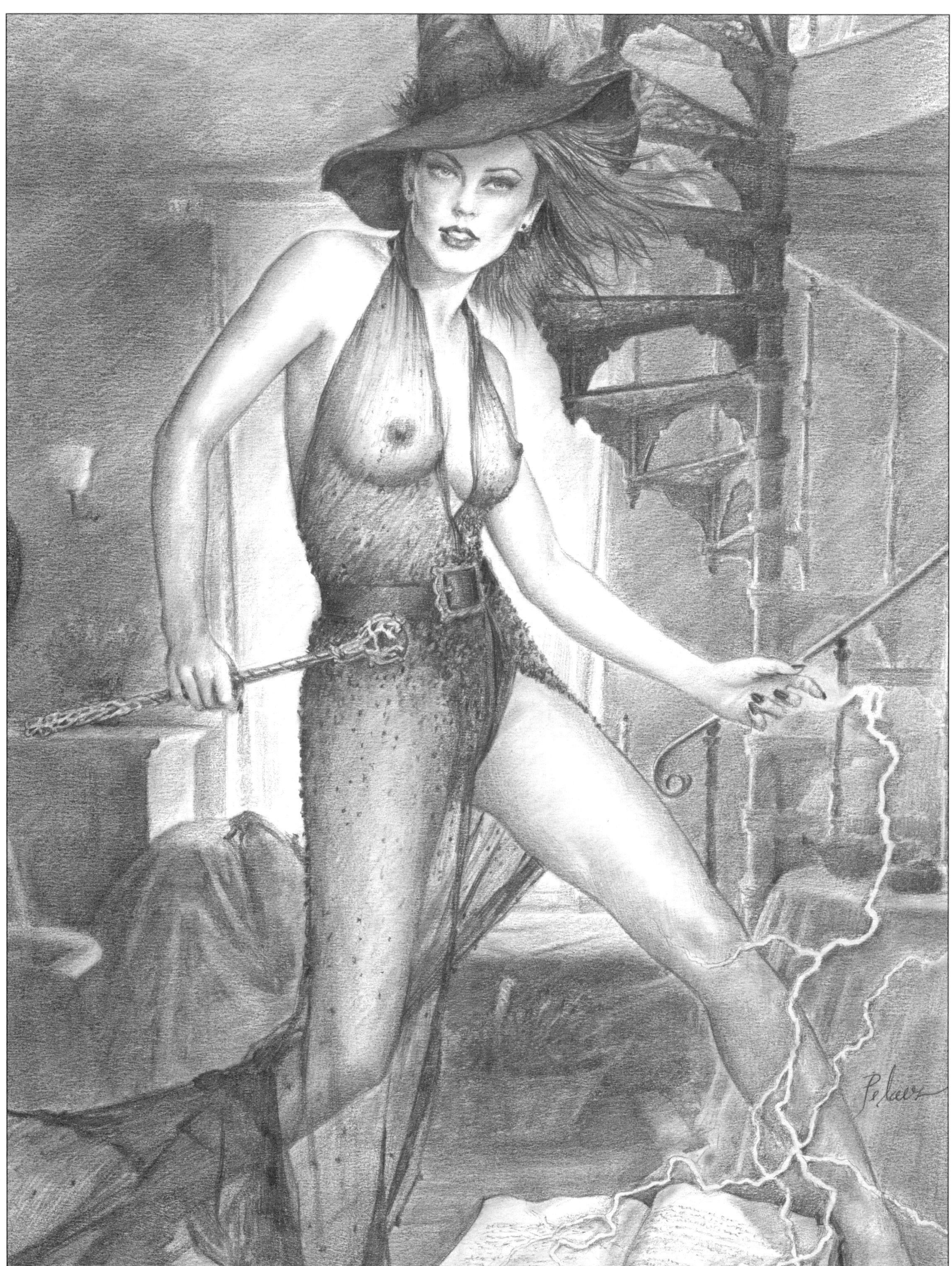
Pelaez

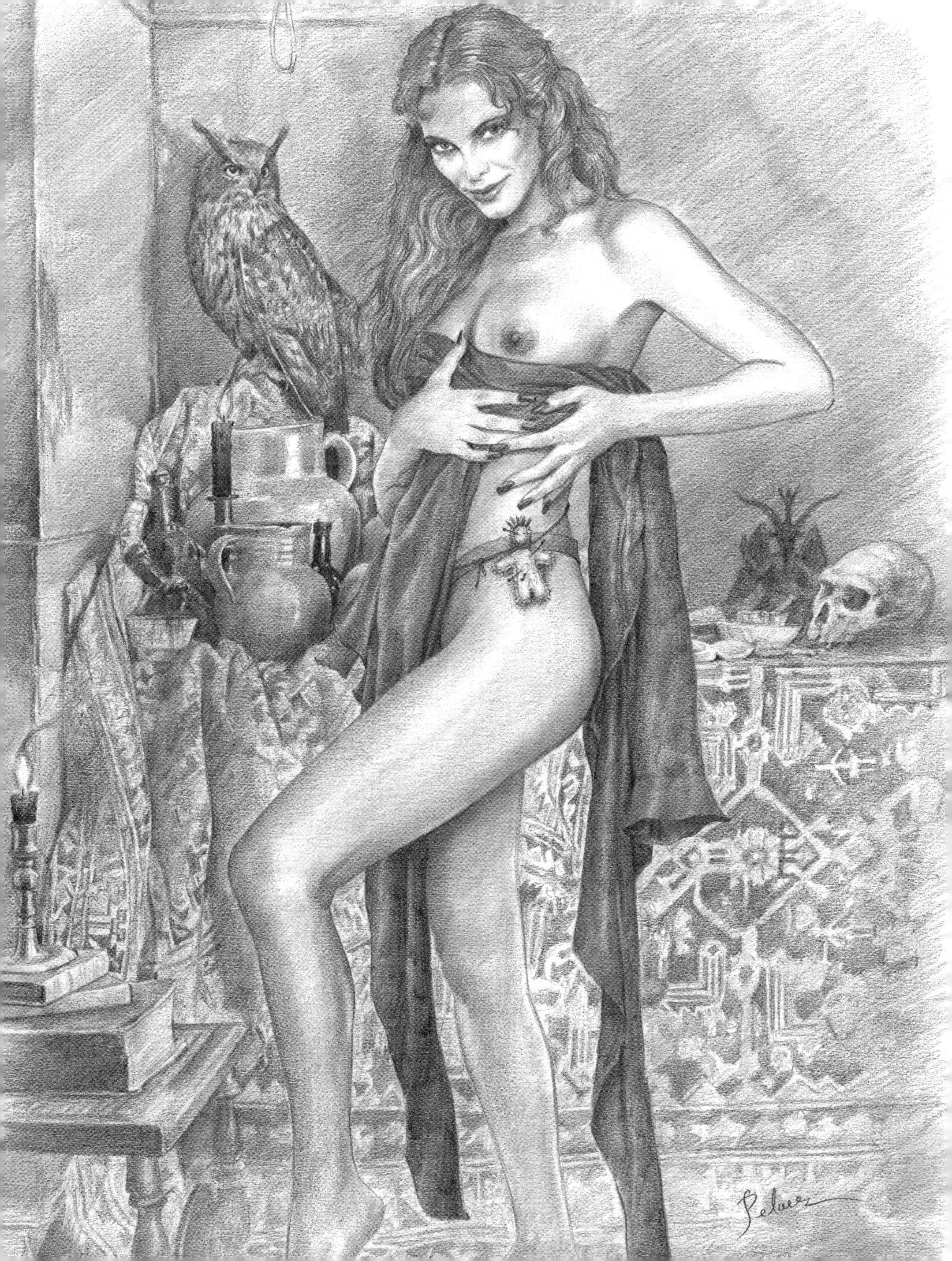

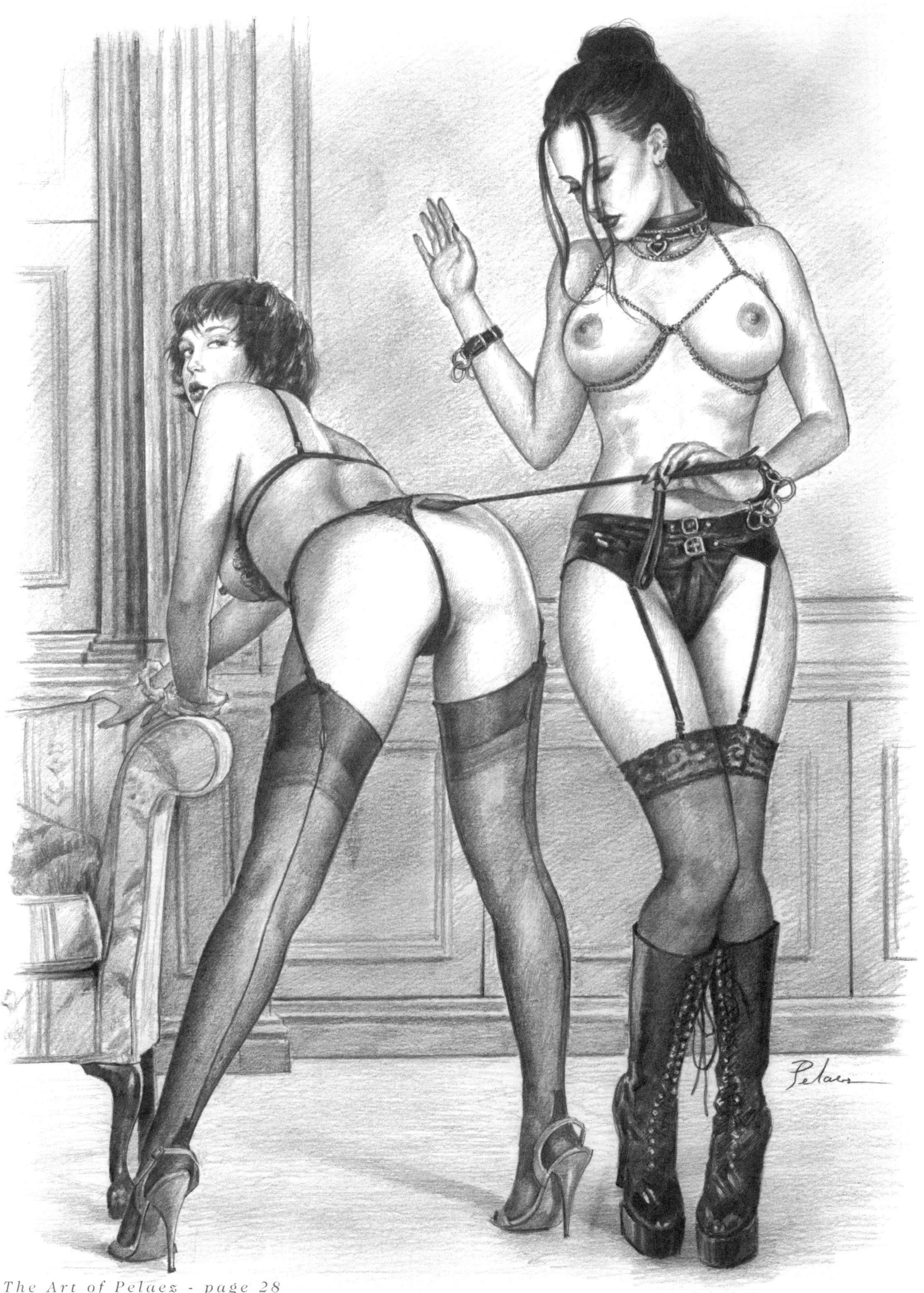
Pelaez

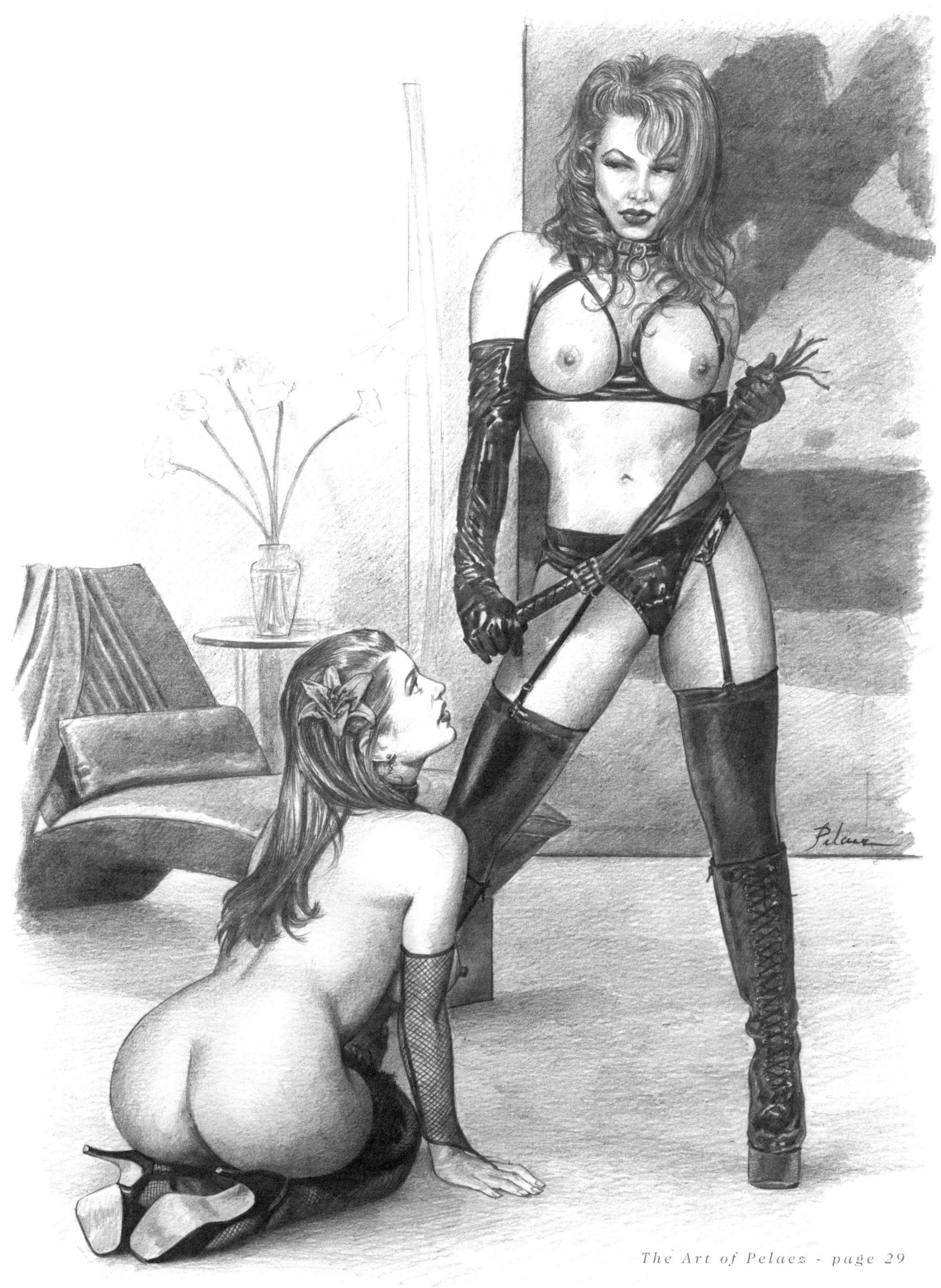

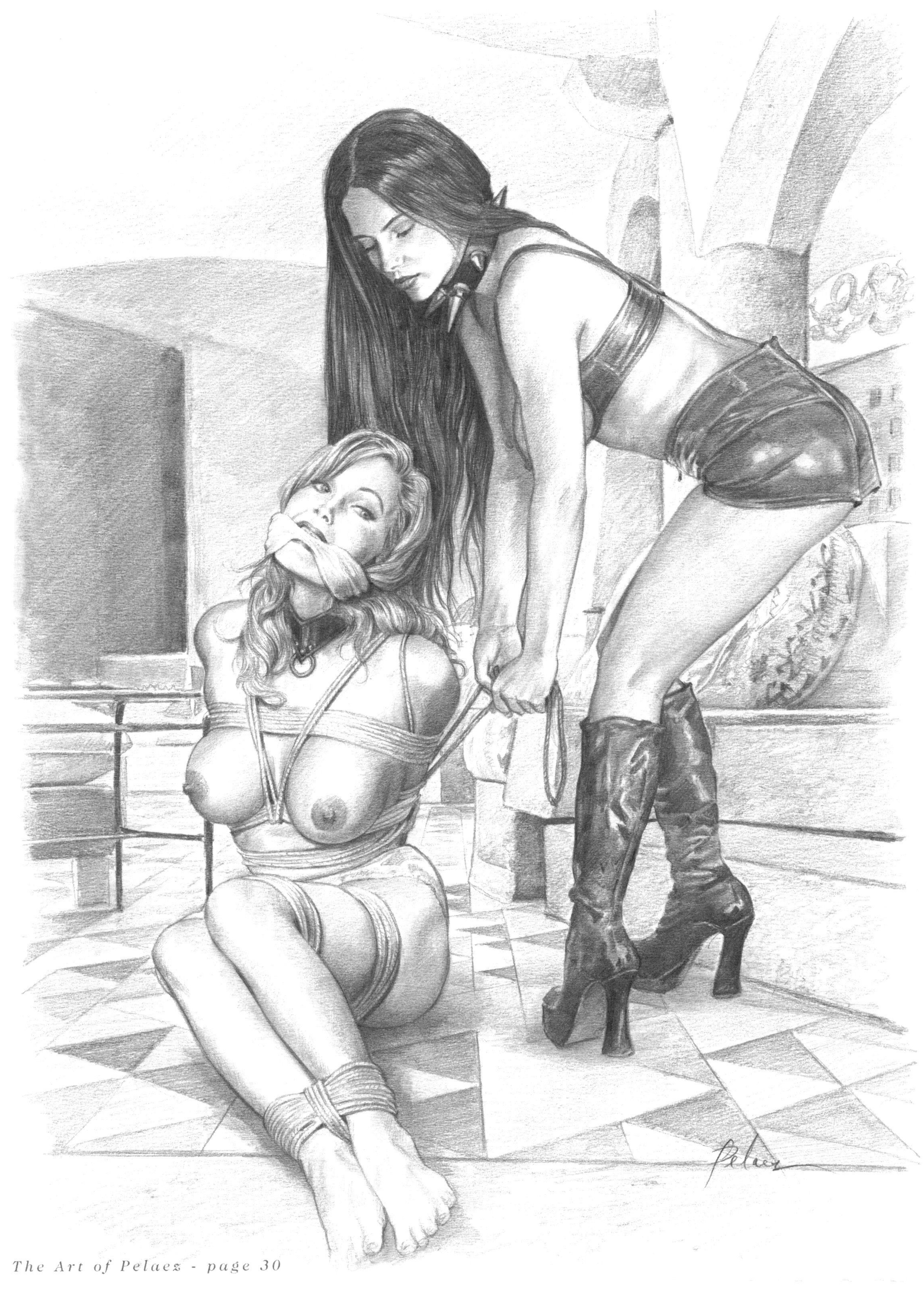
Pelaez

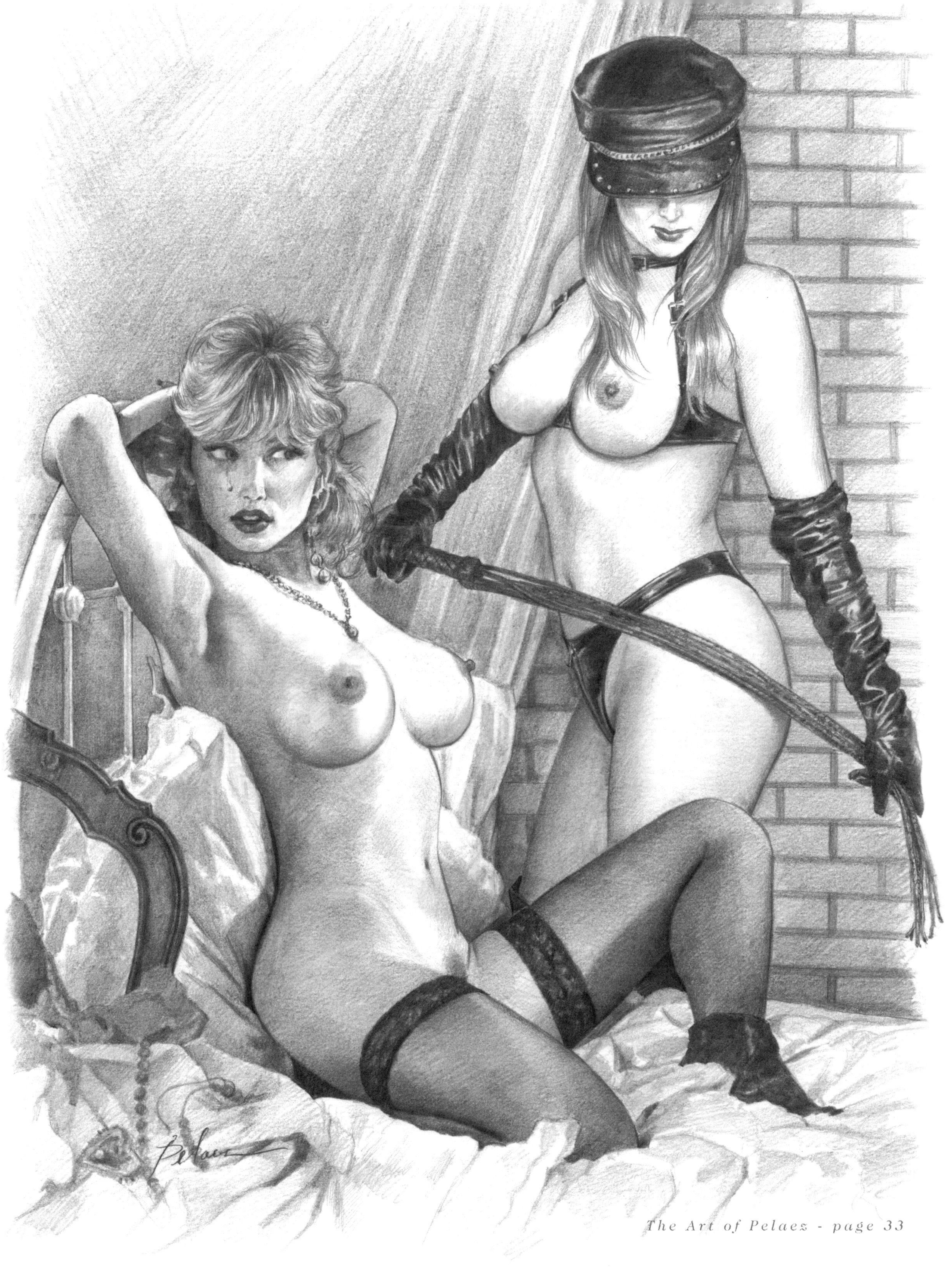
Pelaez

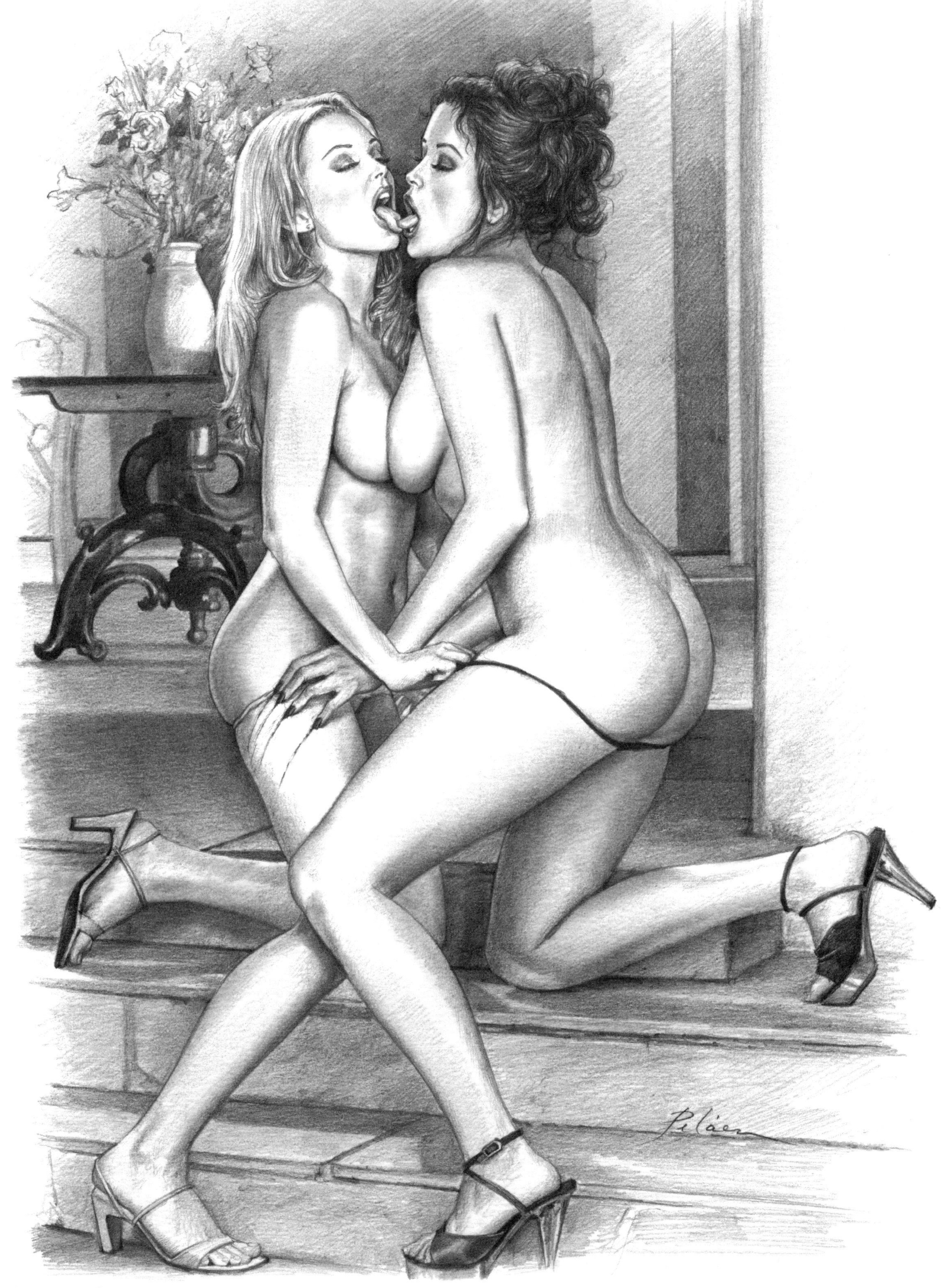

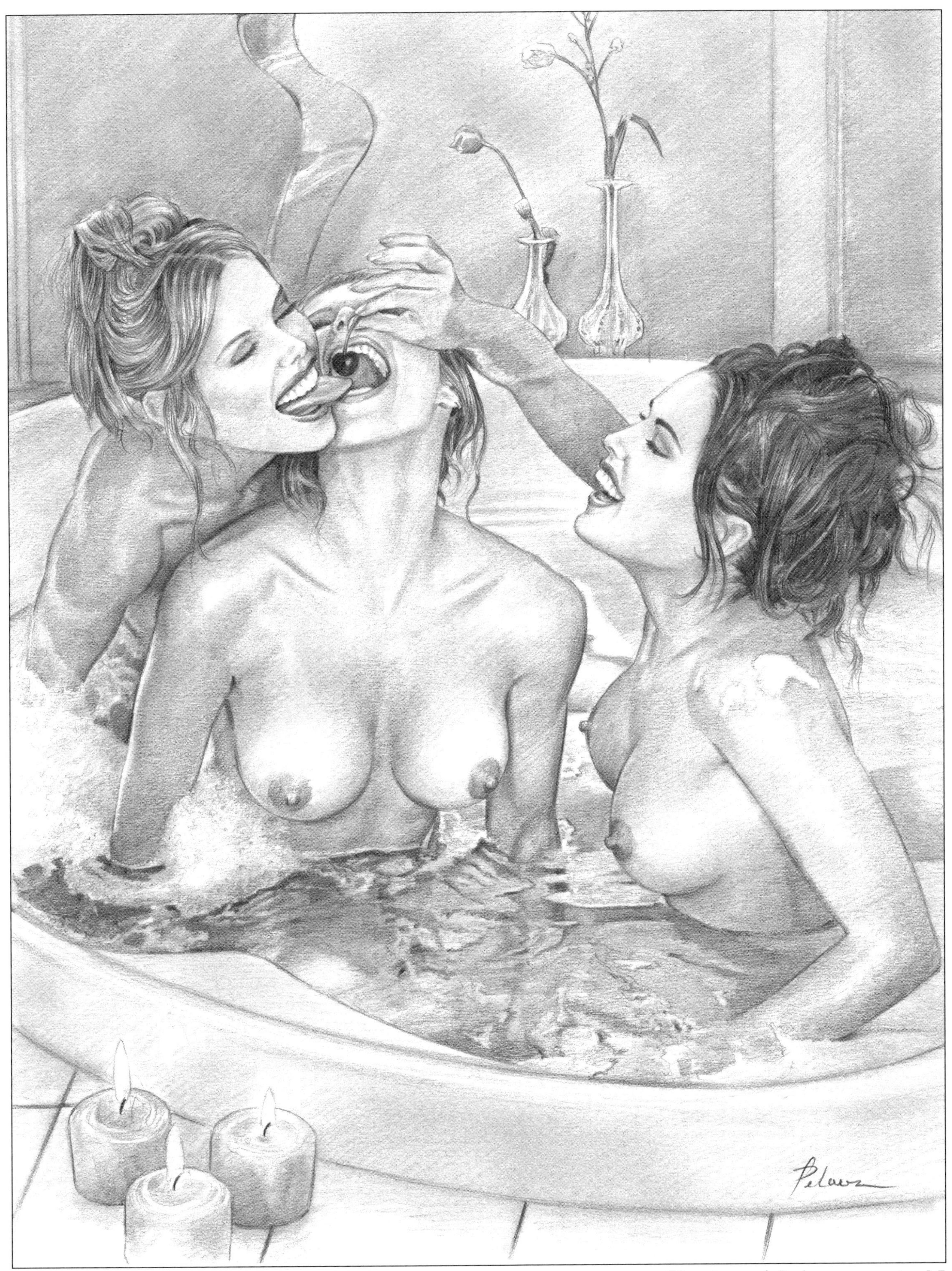
Pelaez

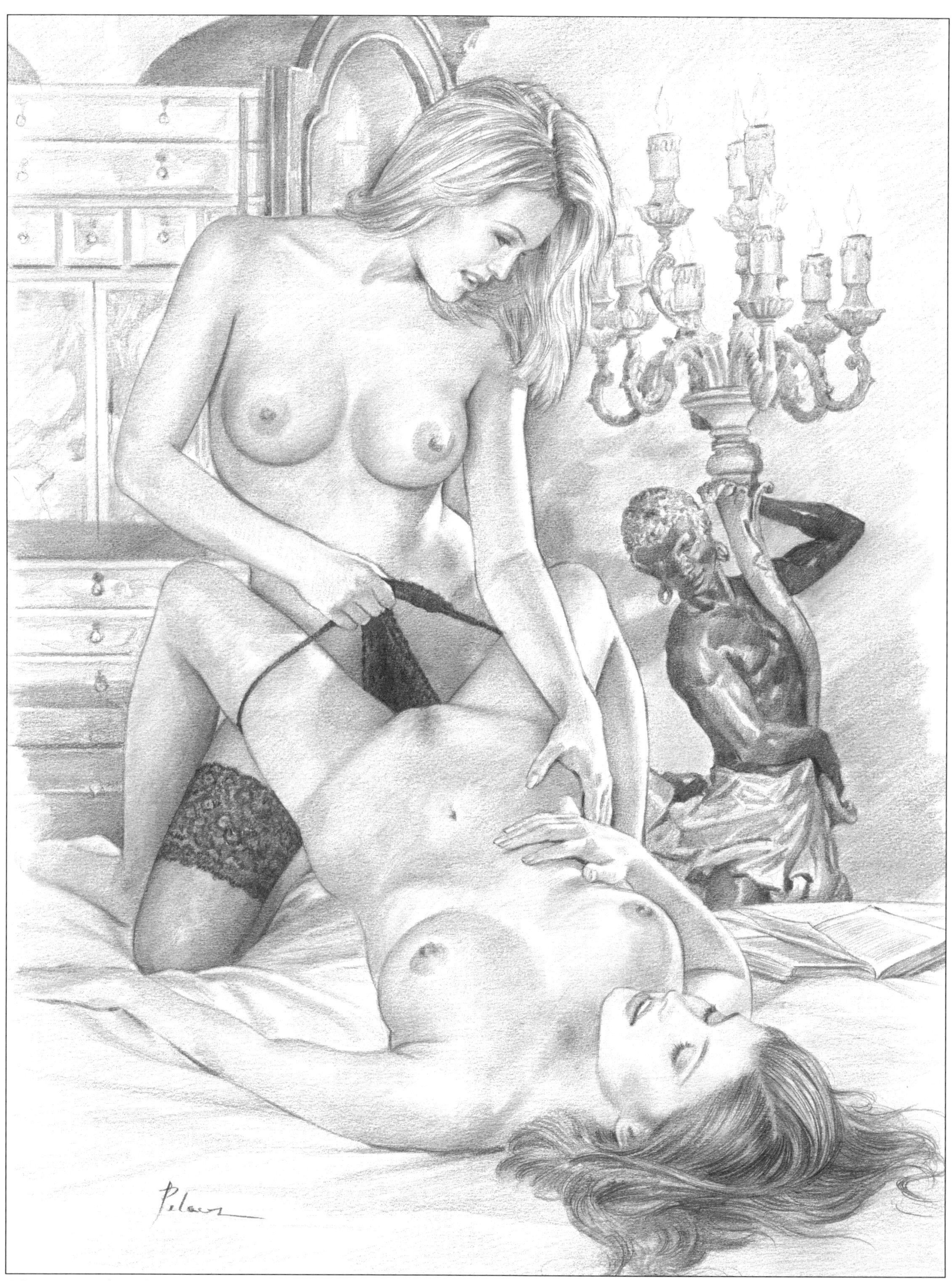

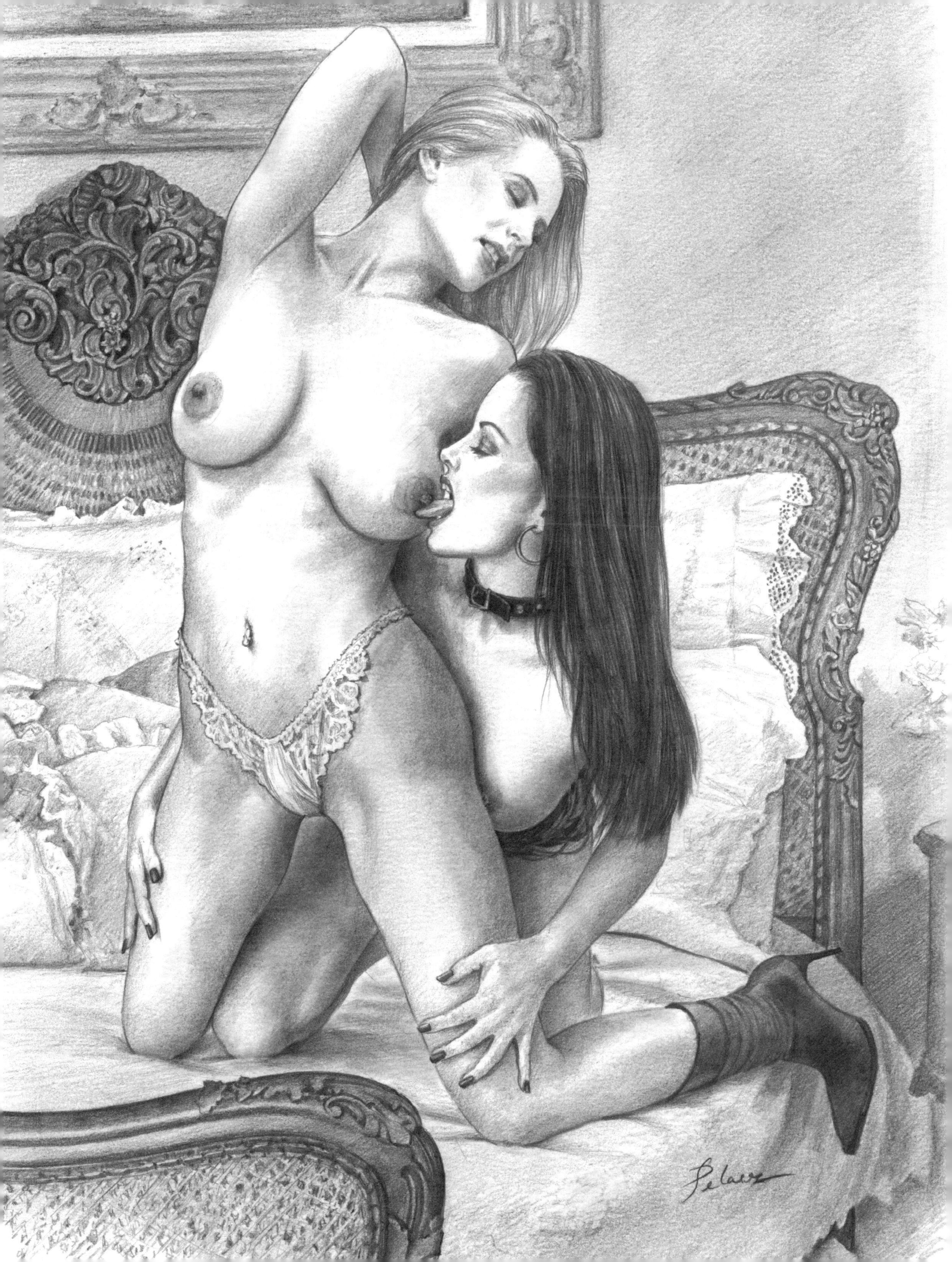

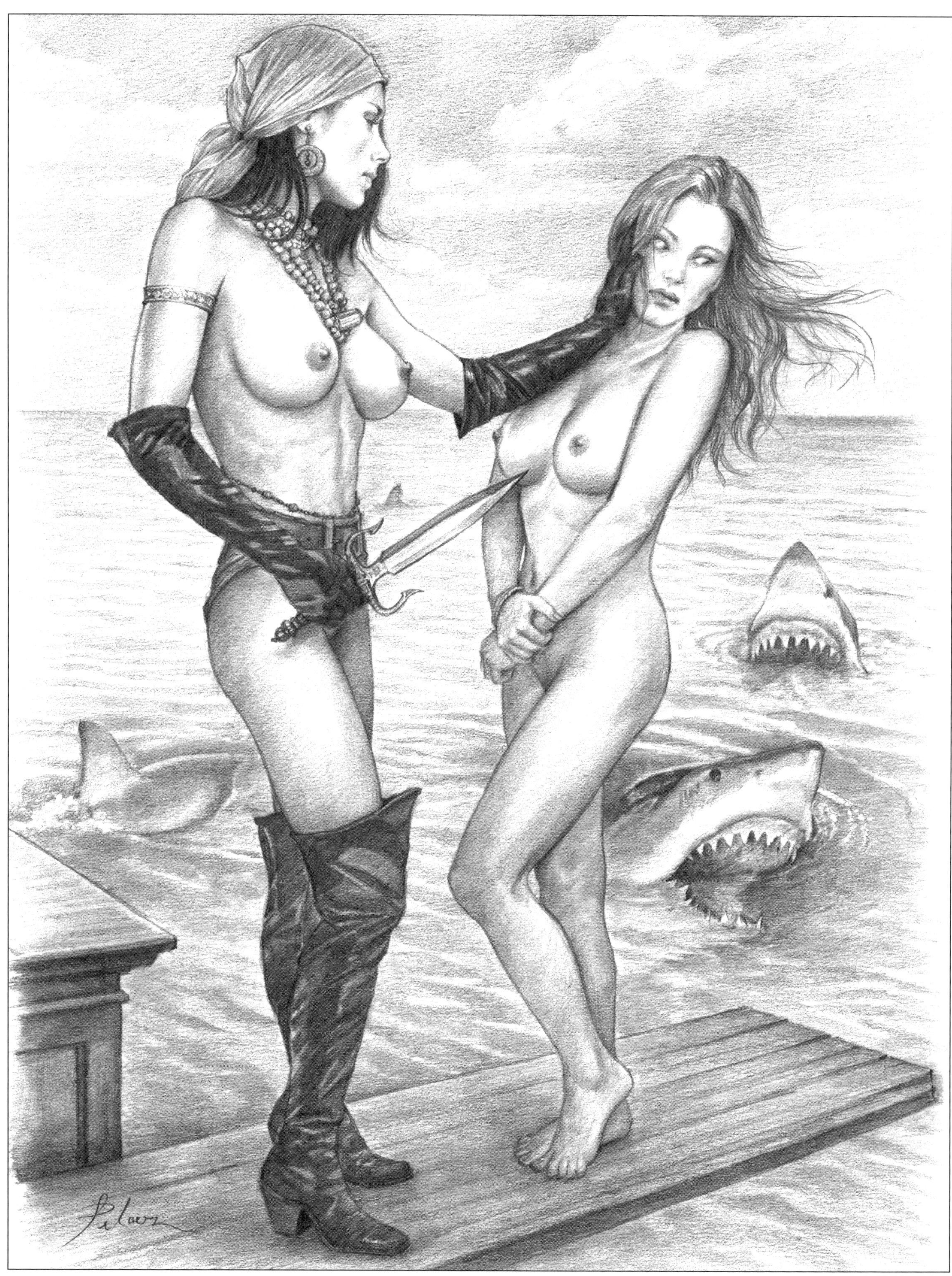

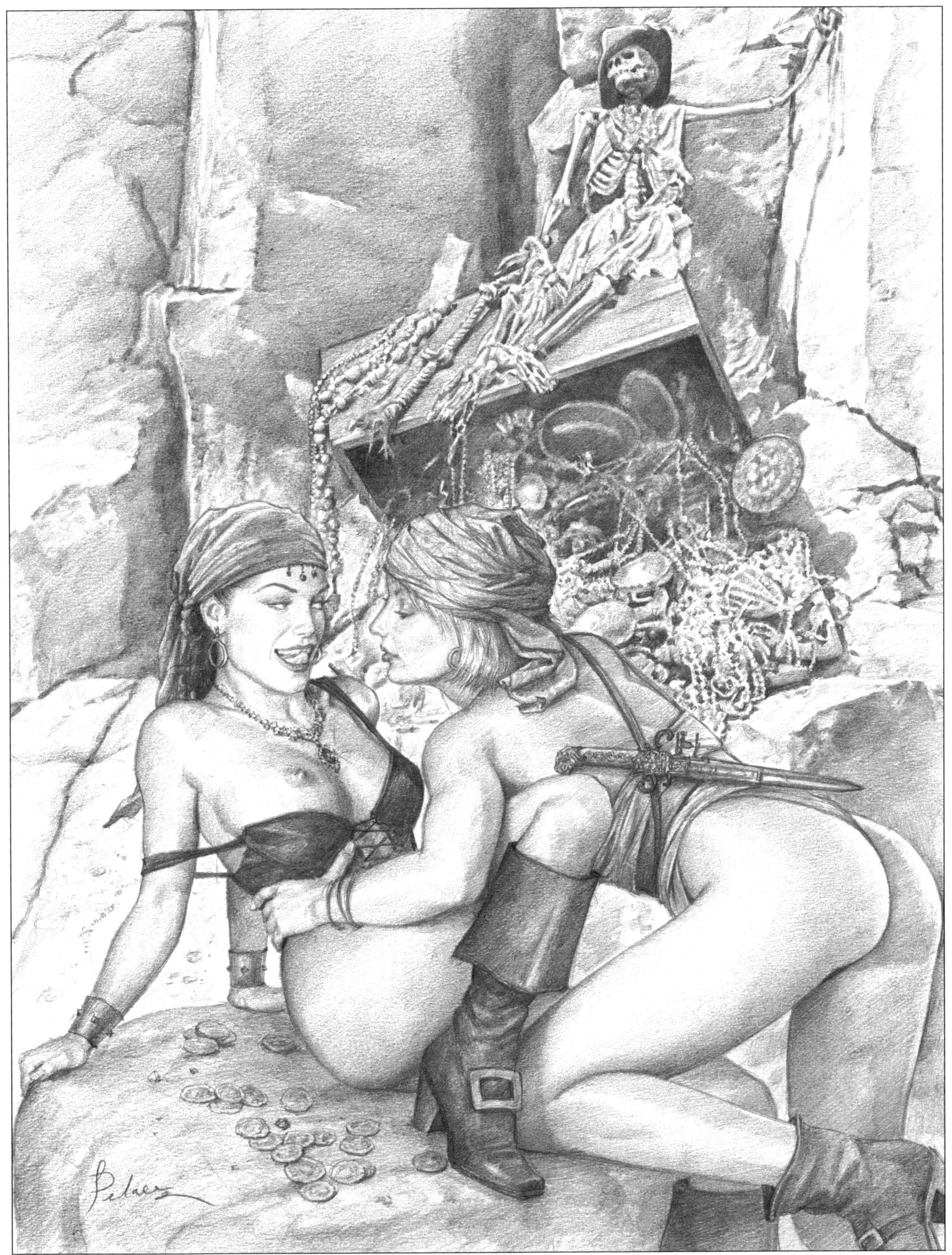
Pelaez

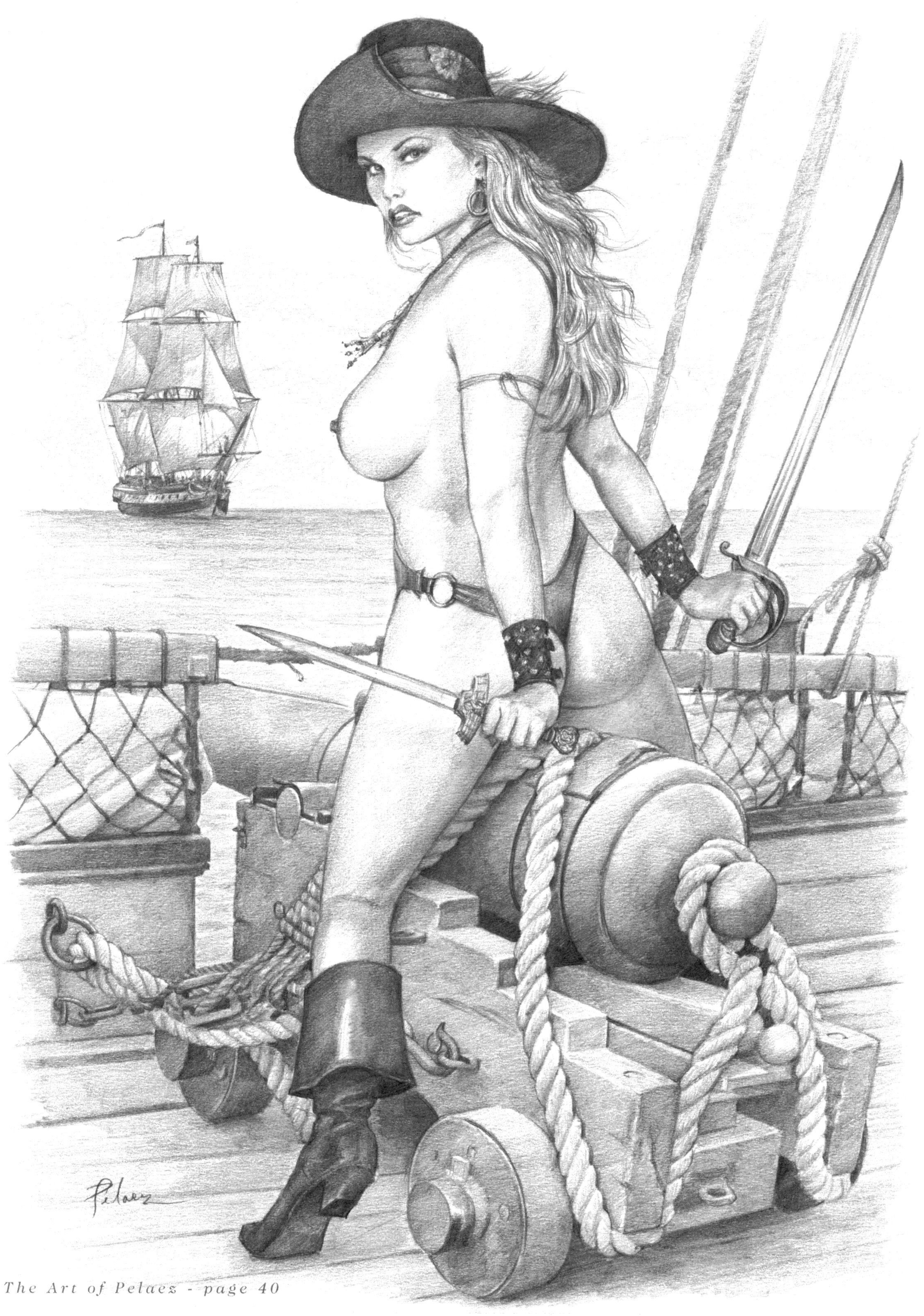
Pelaez

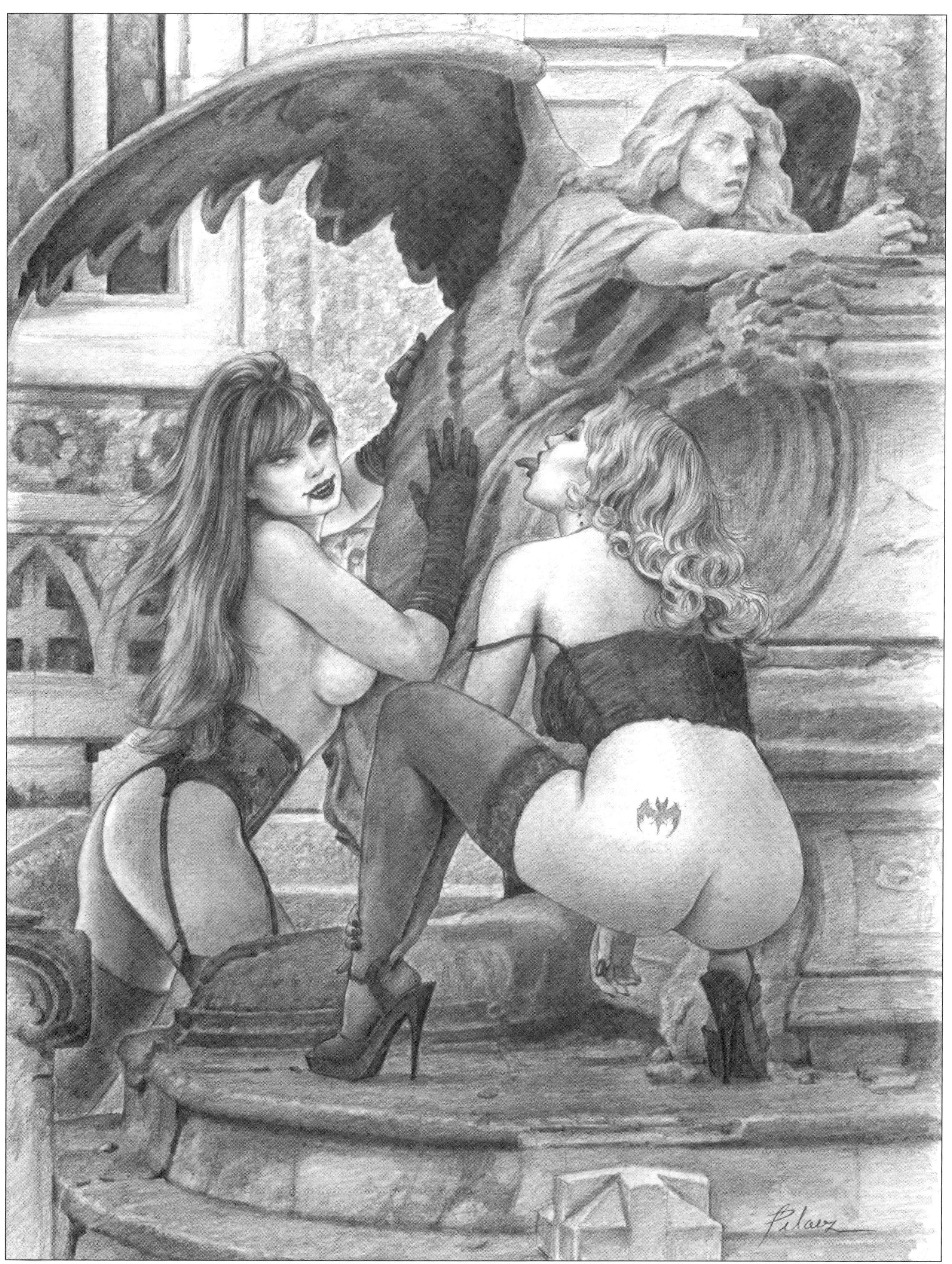

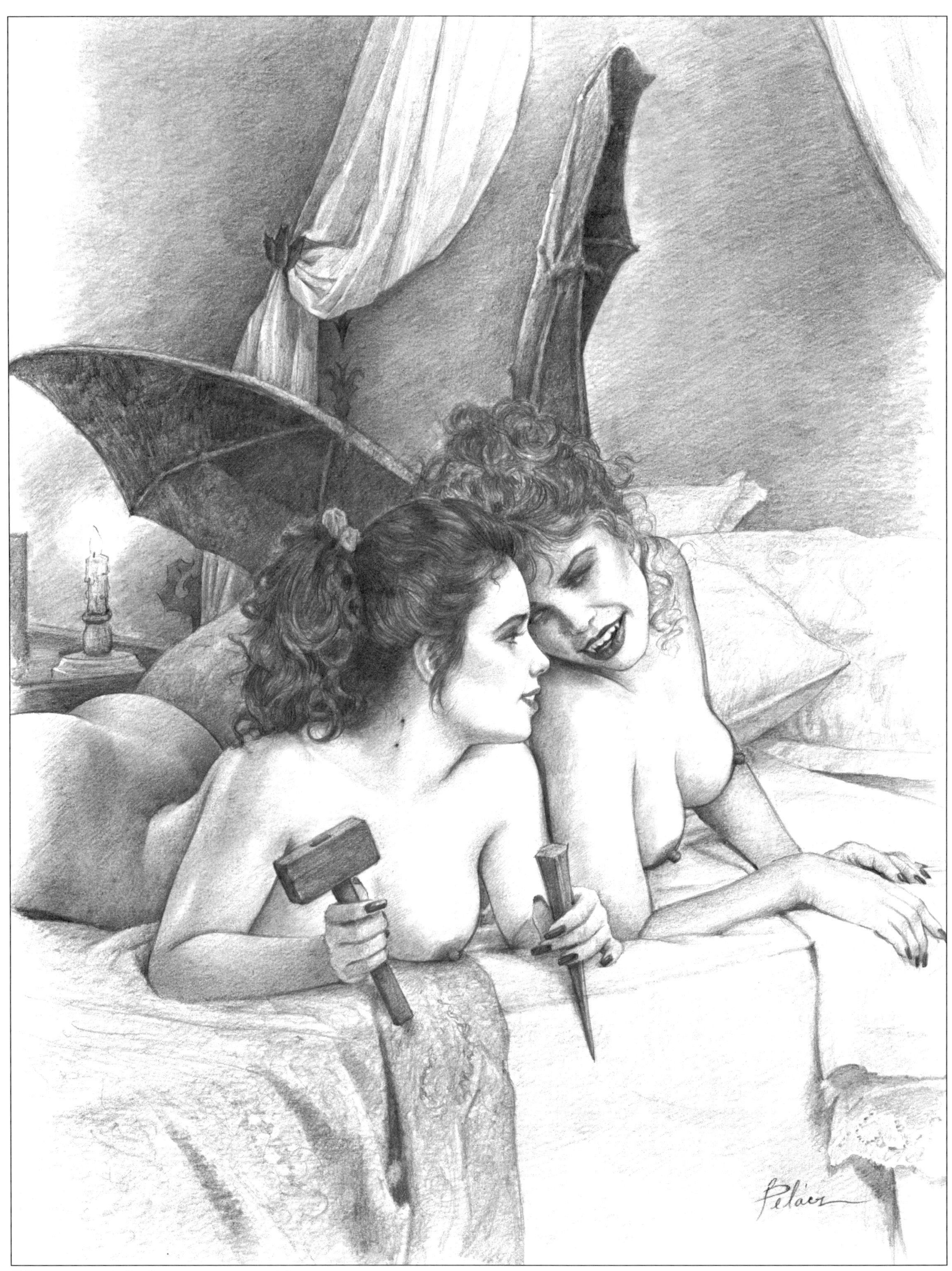
Pelaez

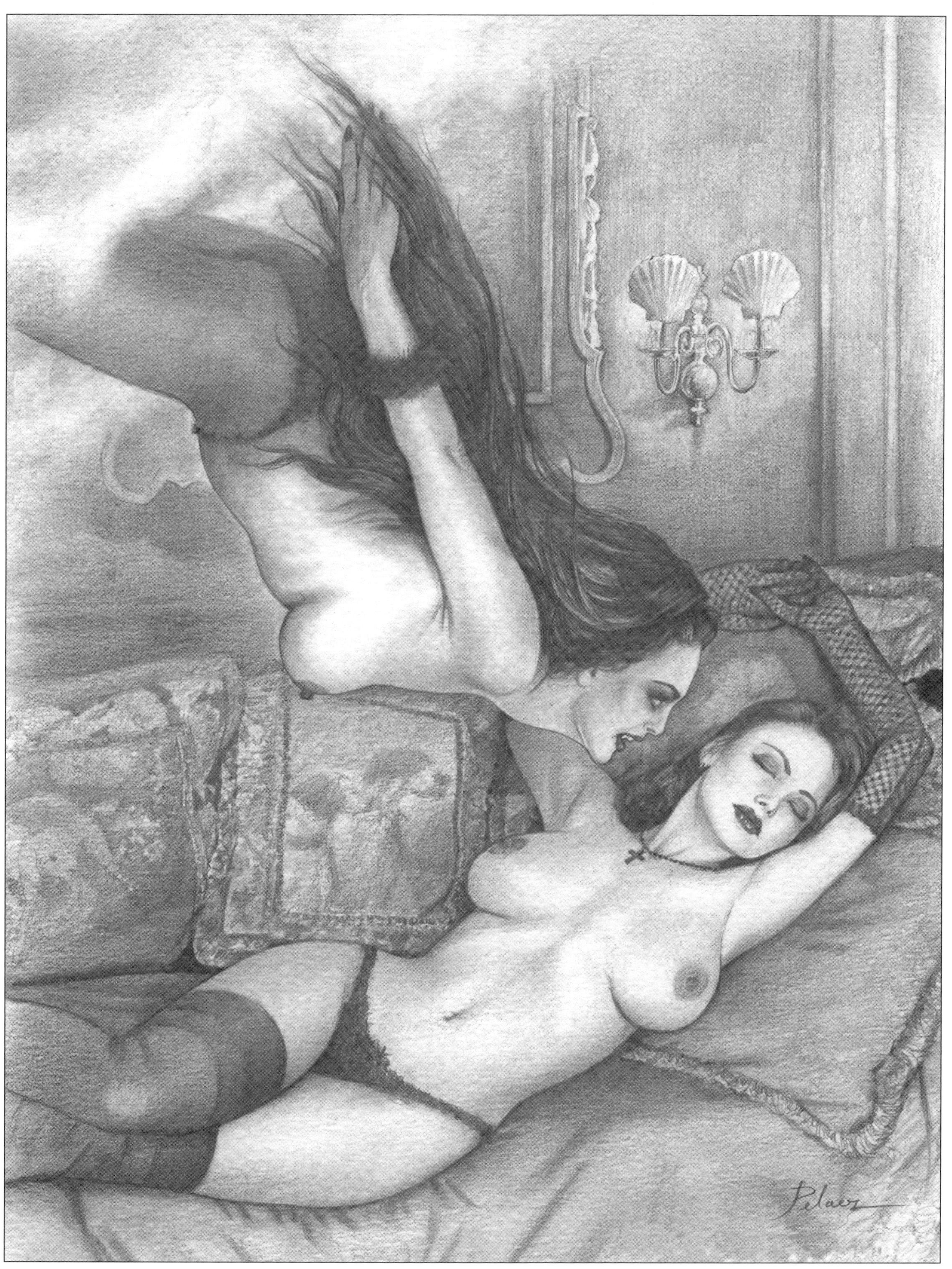
Pelaez

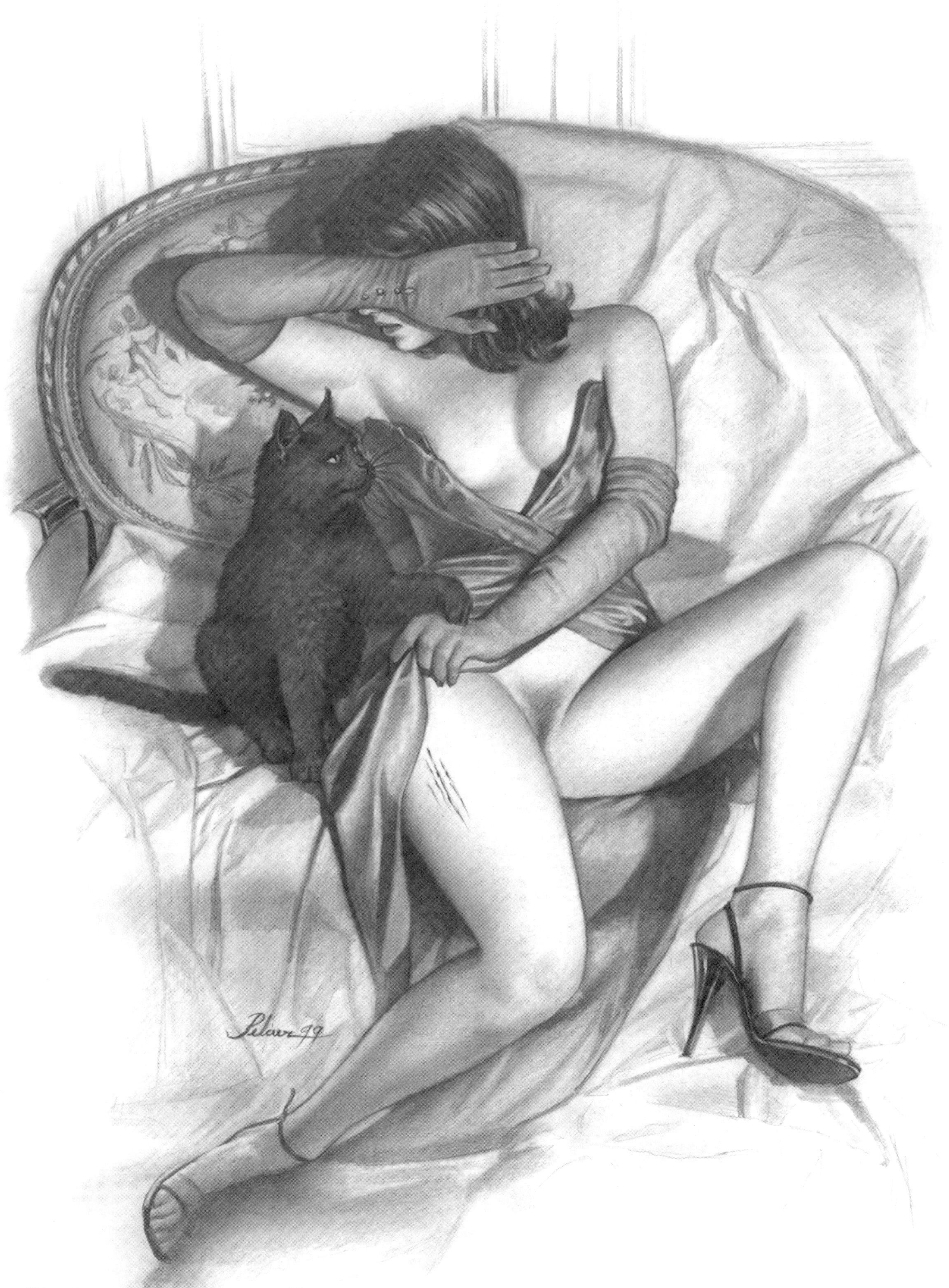
Pelaez 99

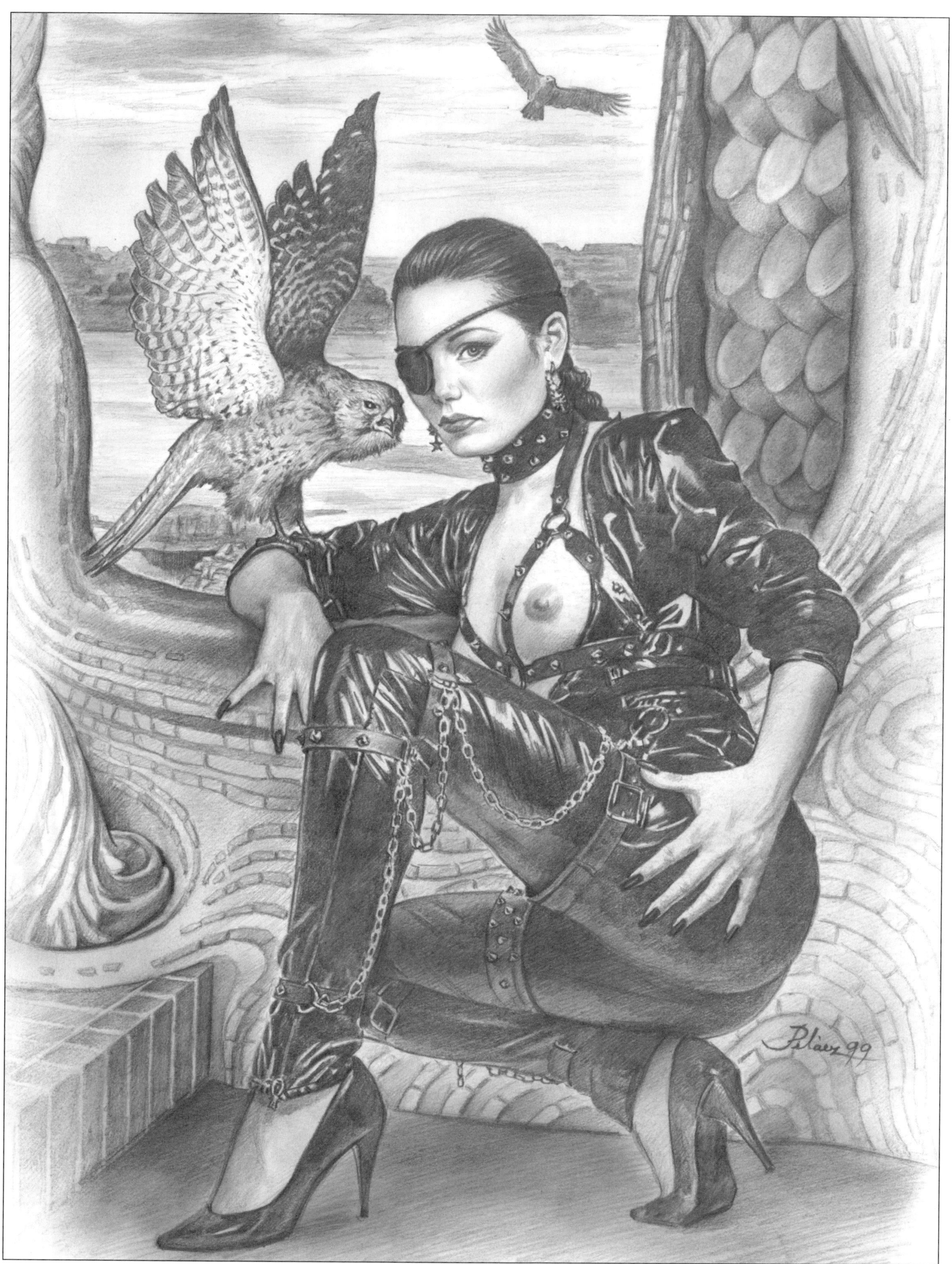
Pelaez 99

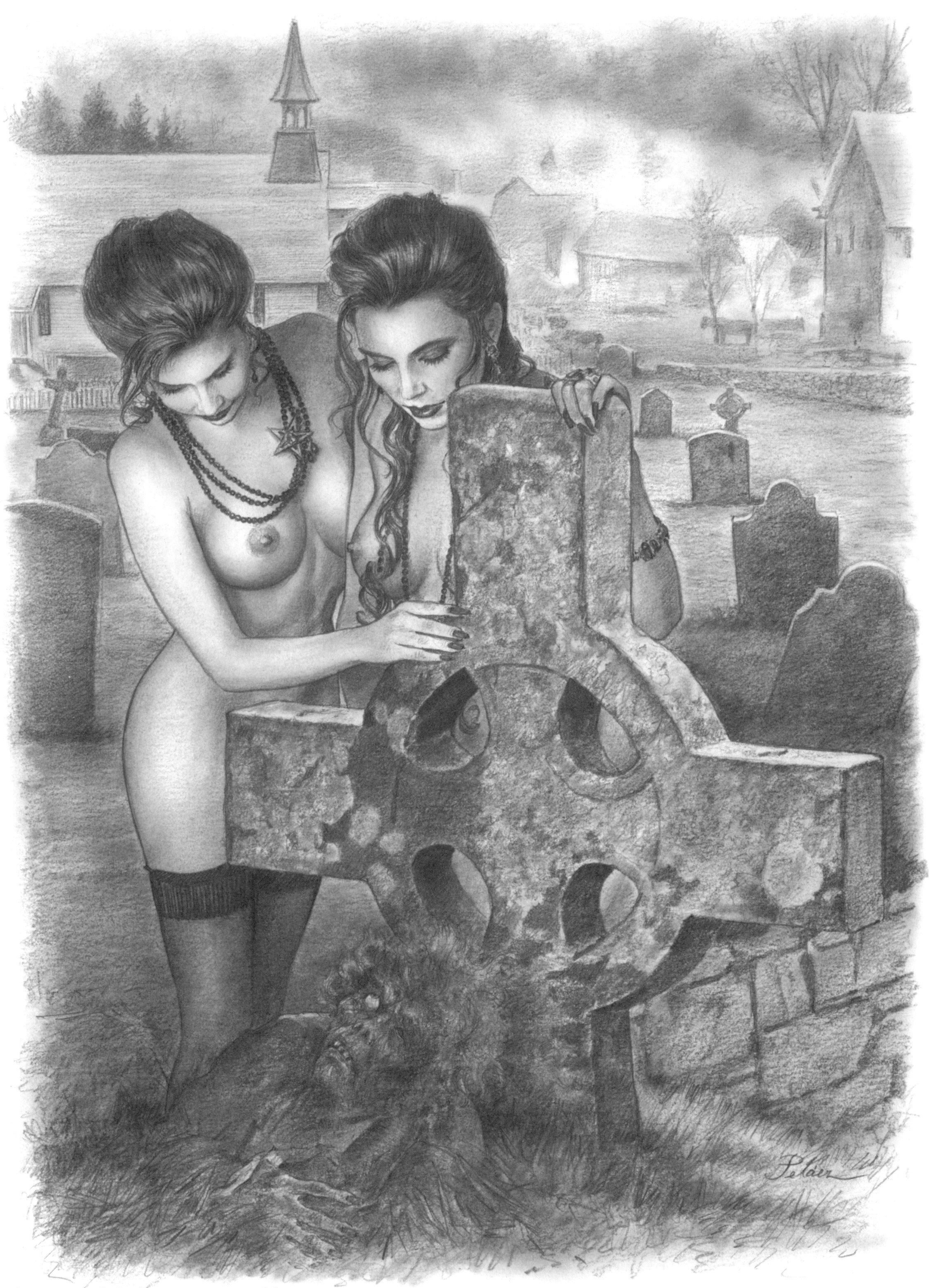
Pelaez

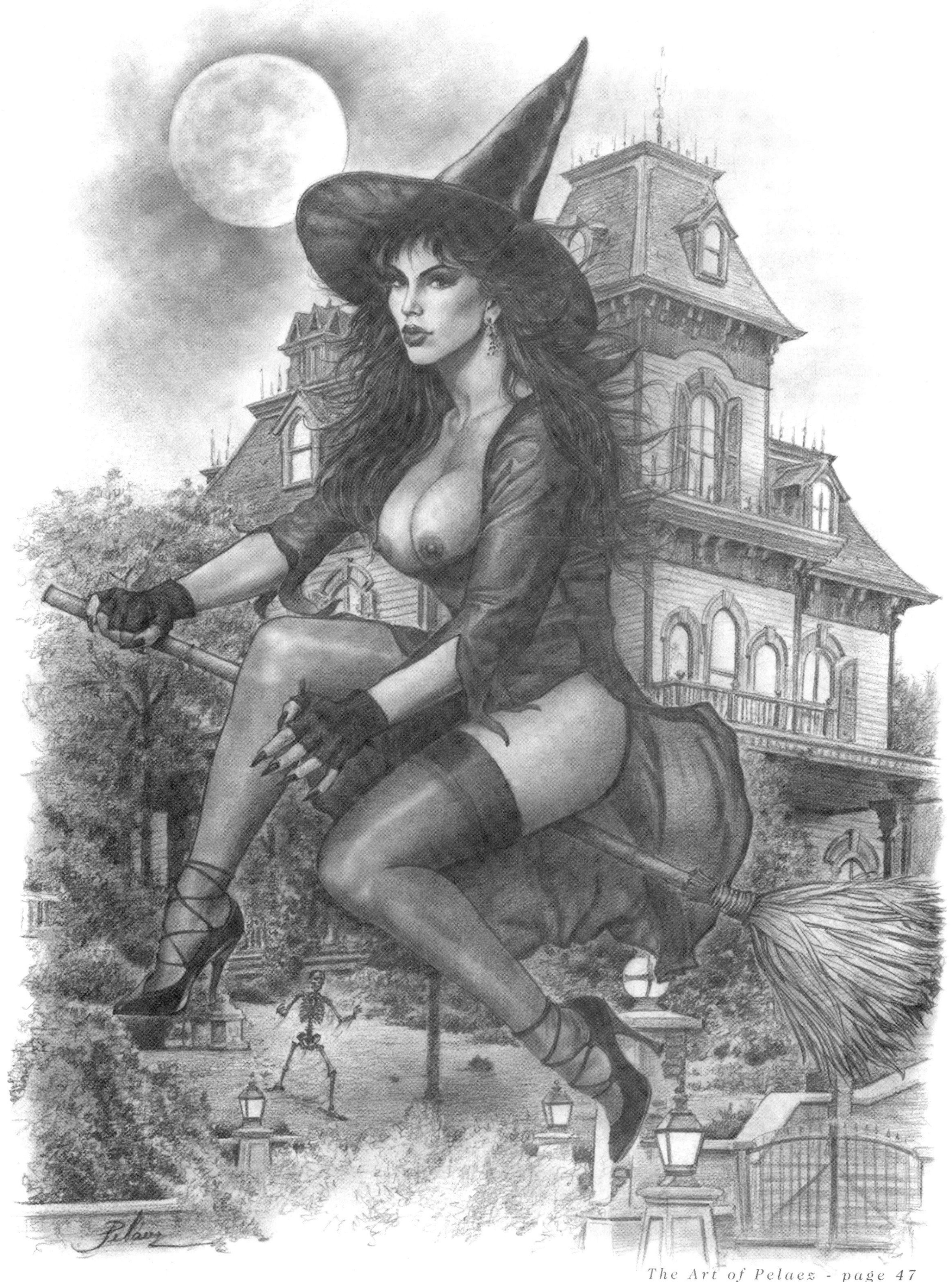
Pelaez

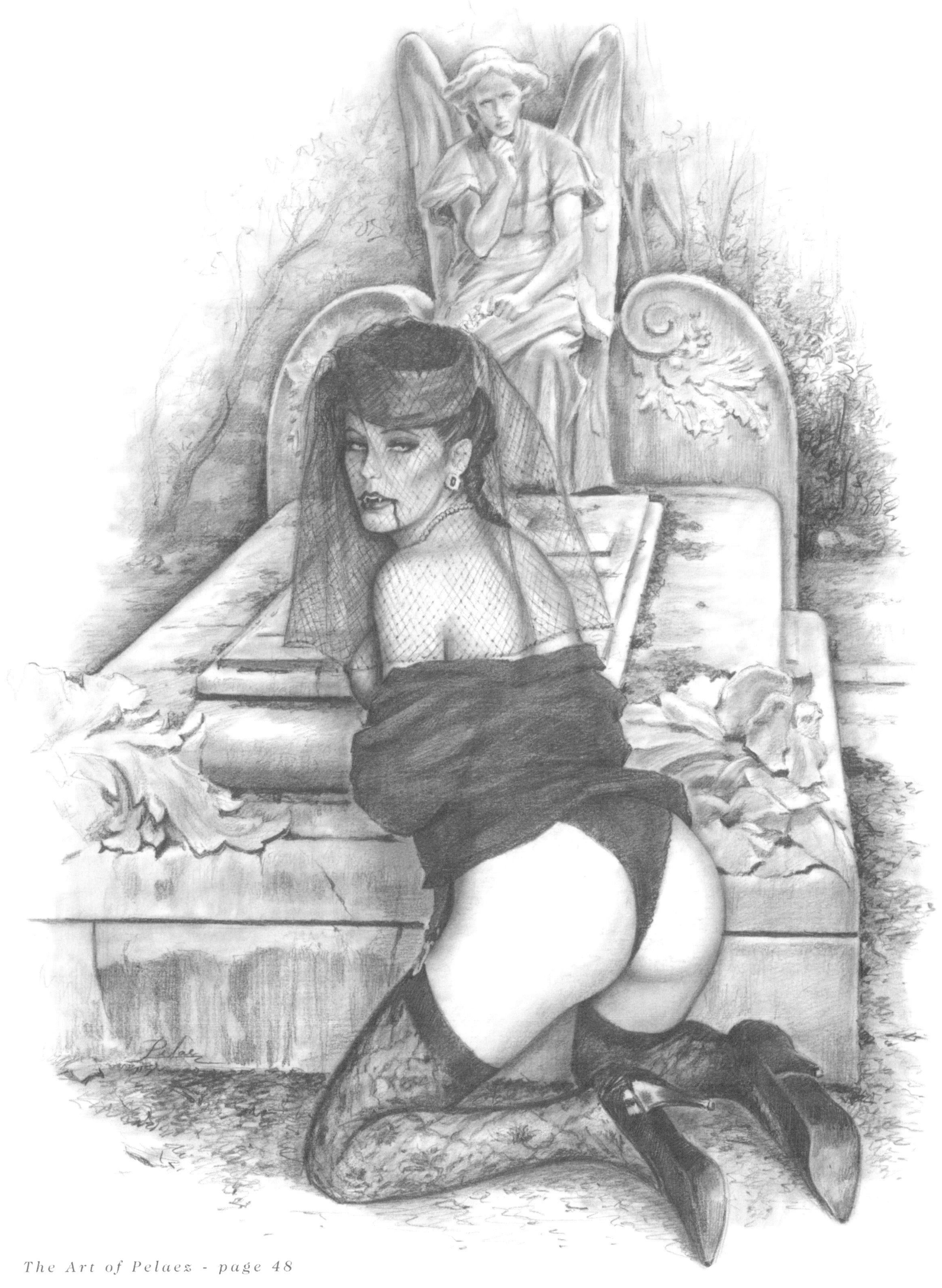

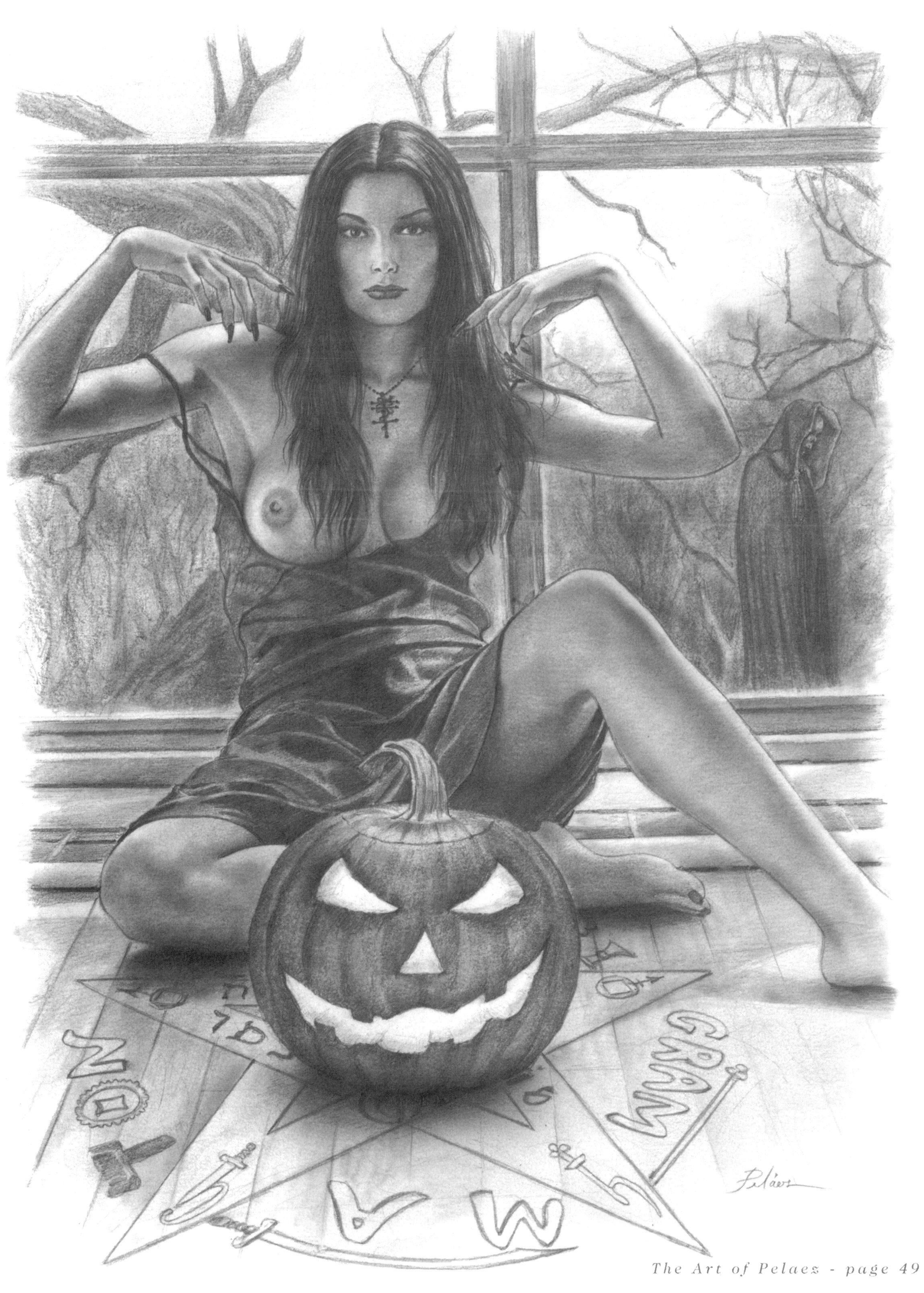

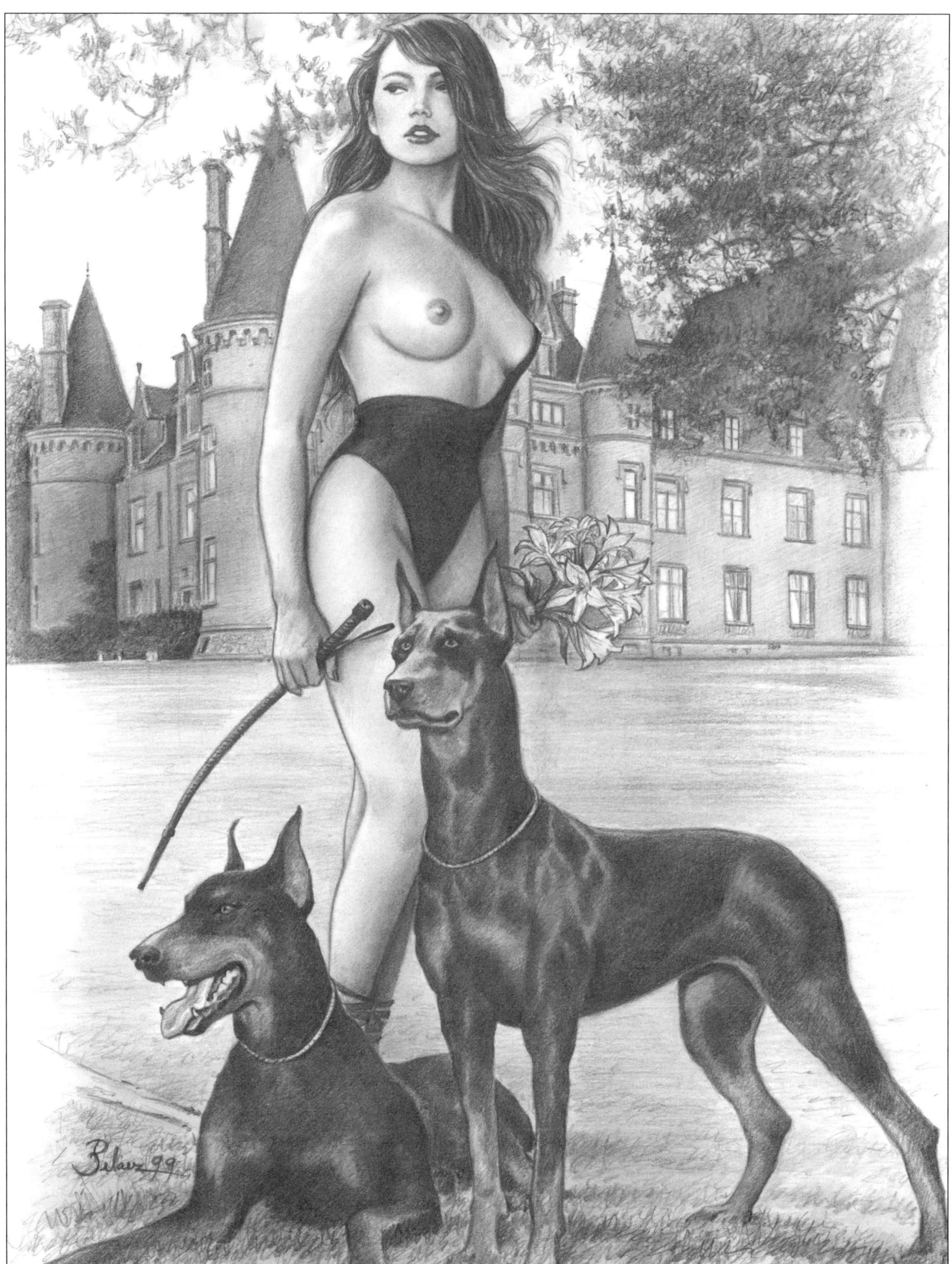
Pelaez 99

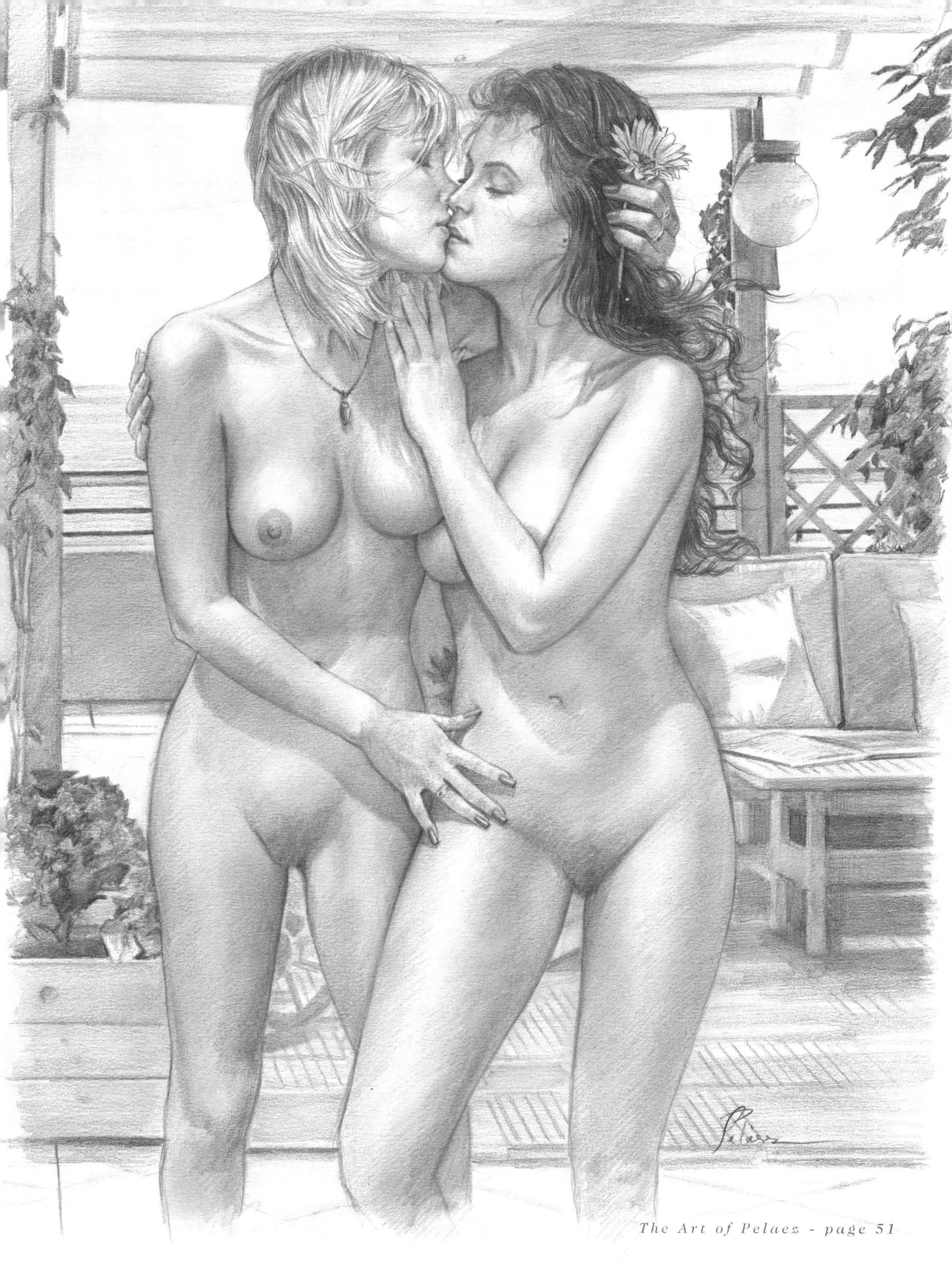

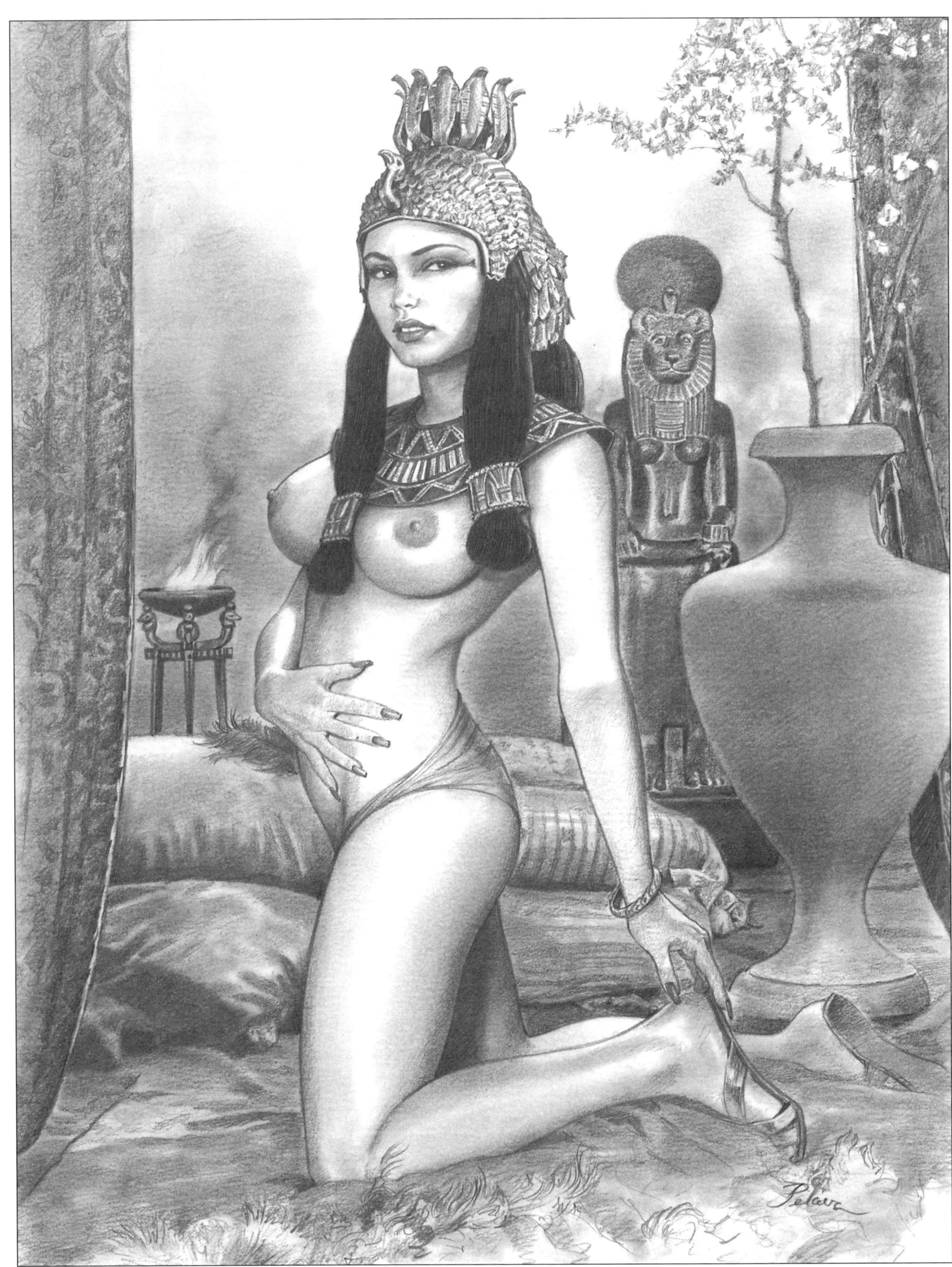
Pelaez

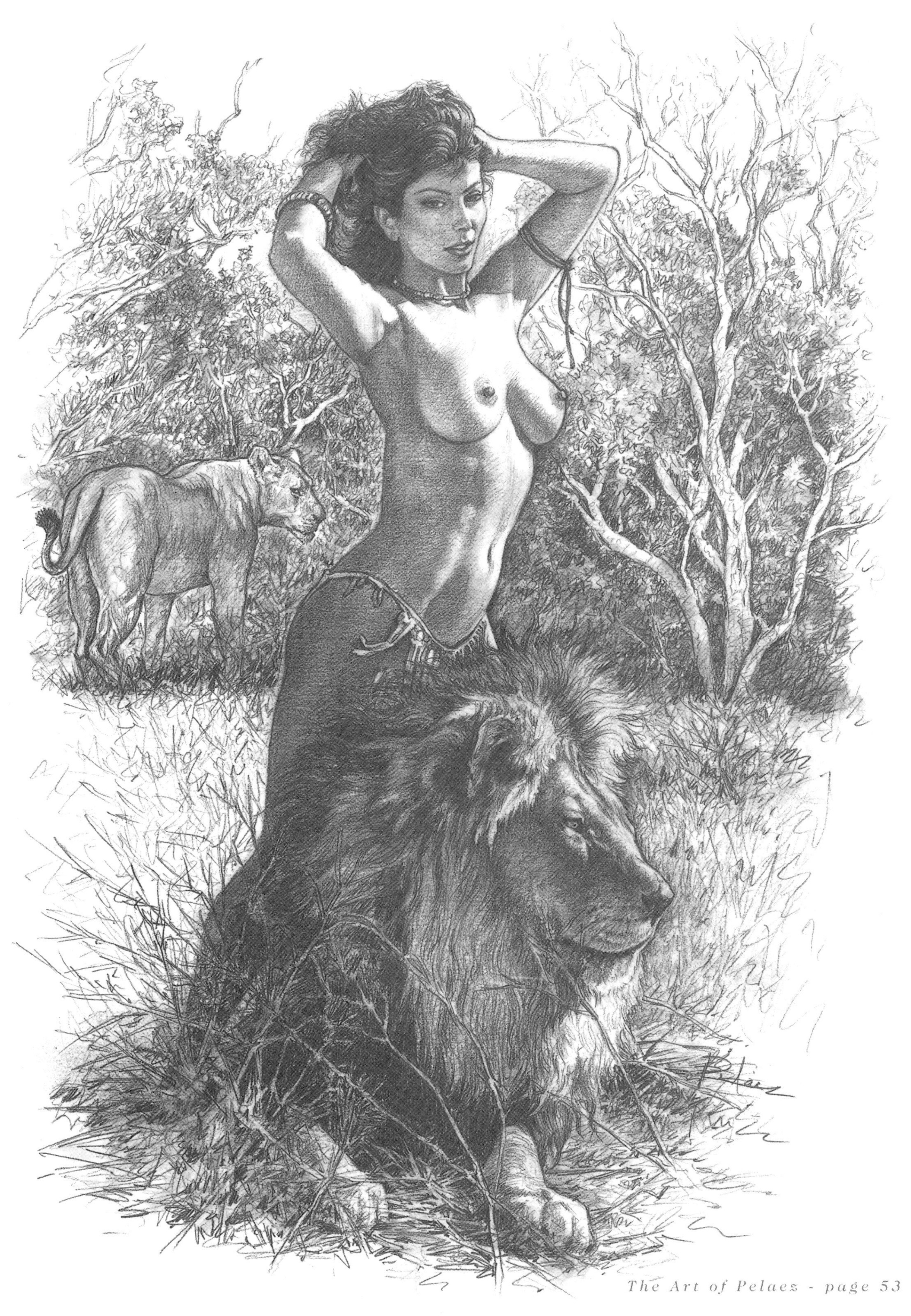

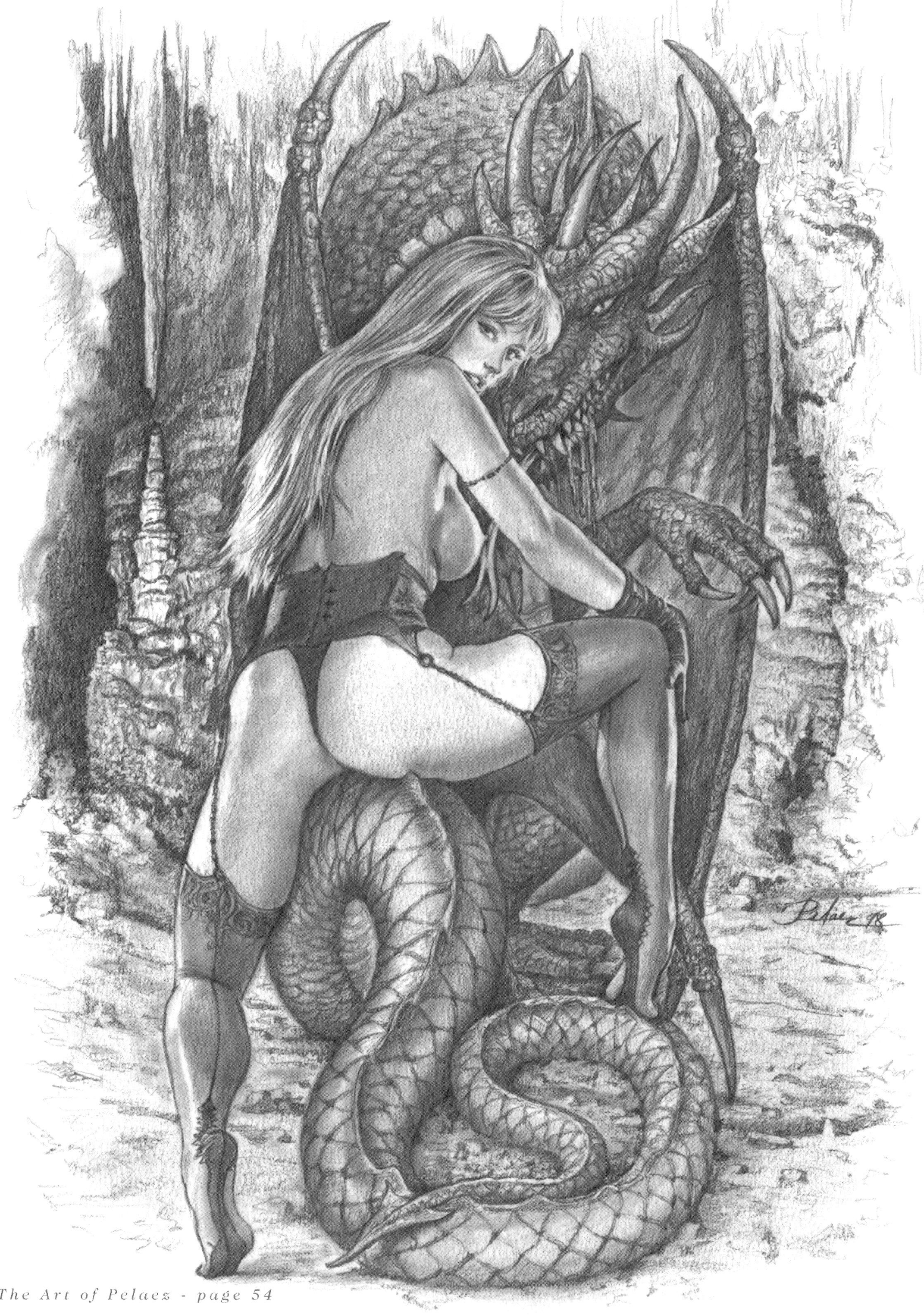

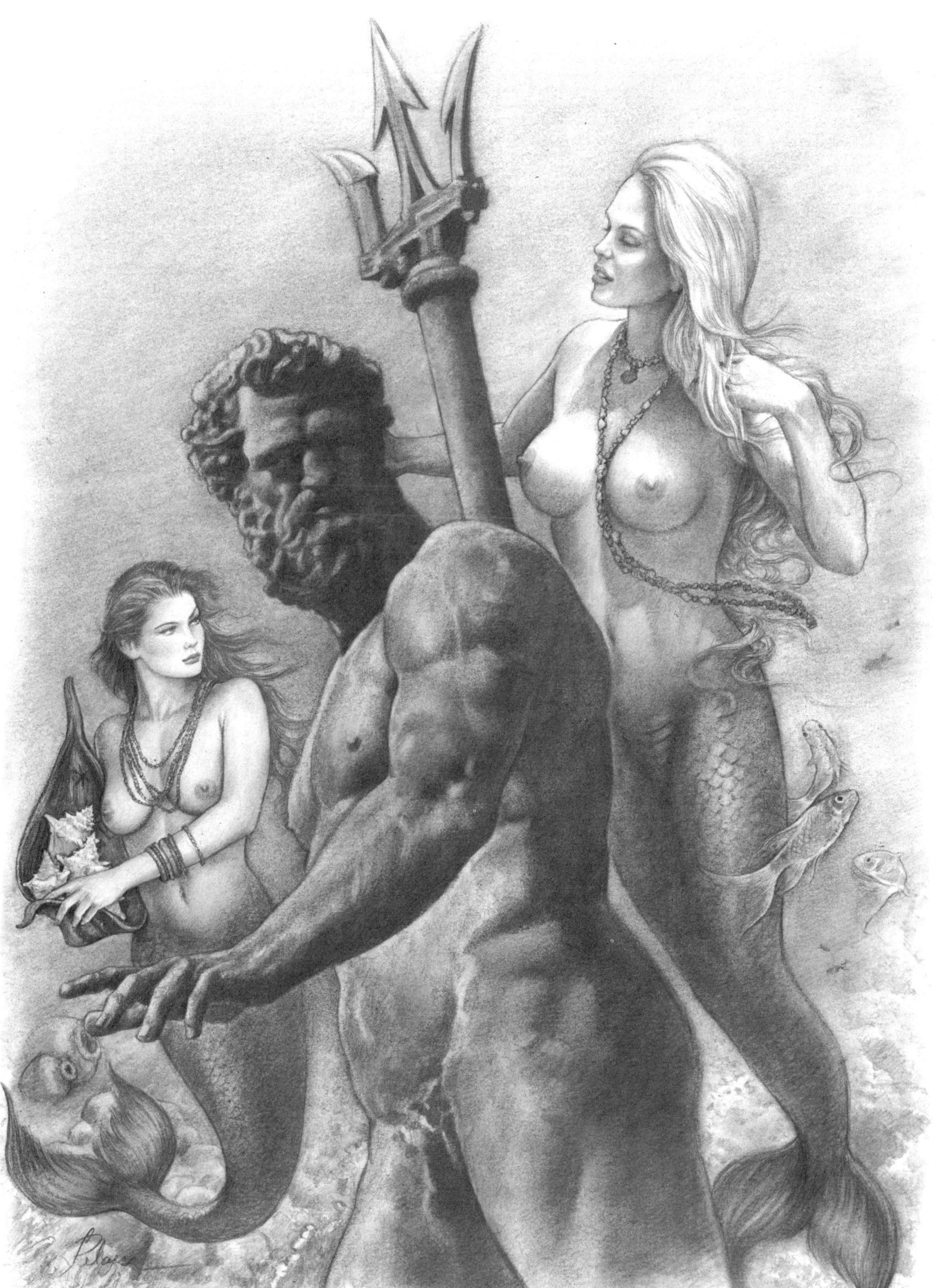

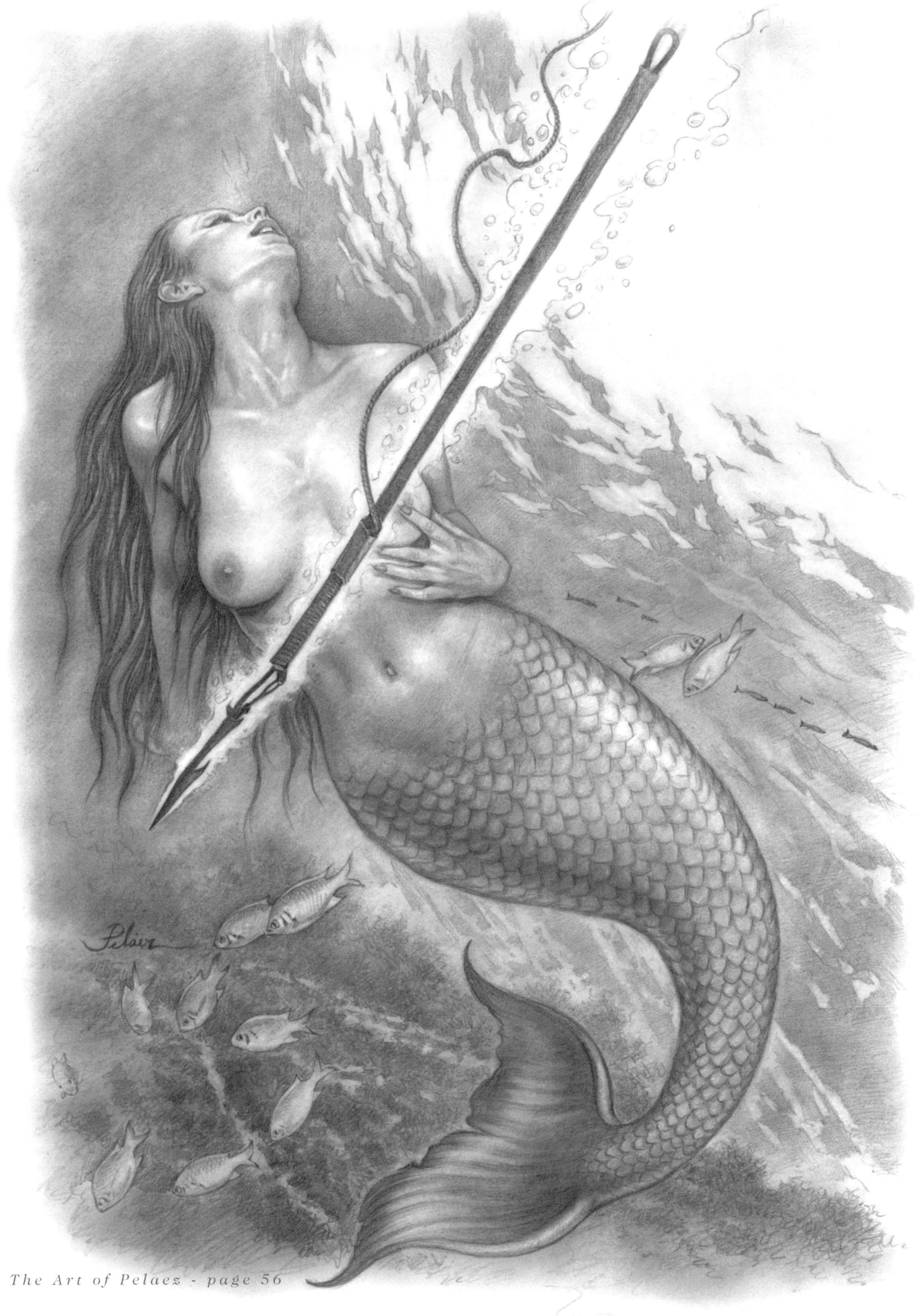
Pelaez

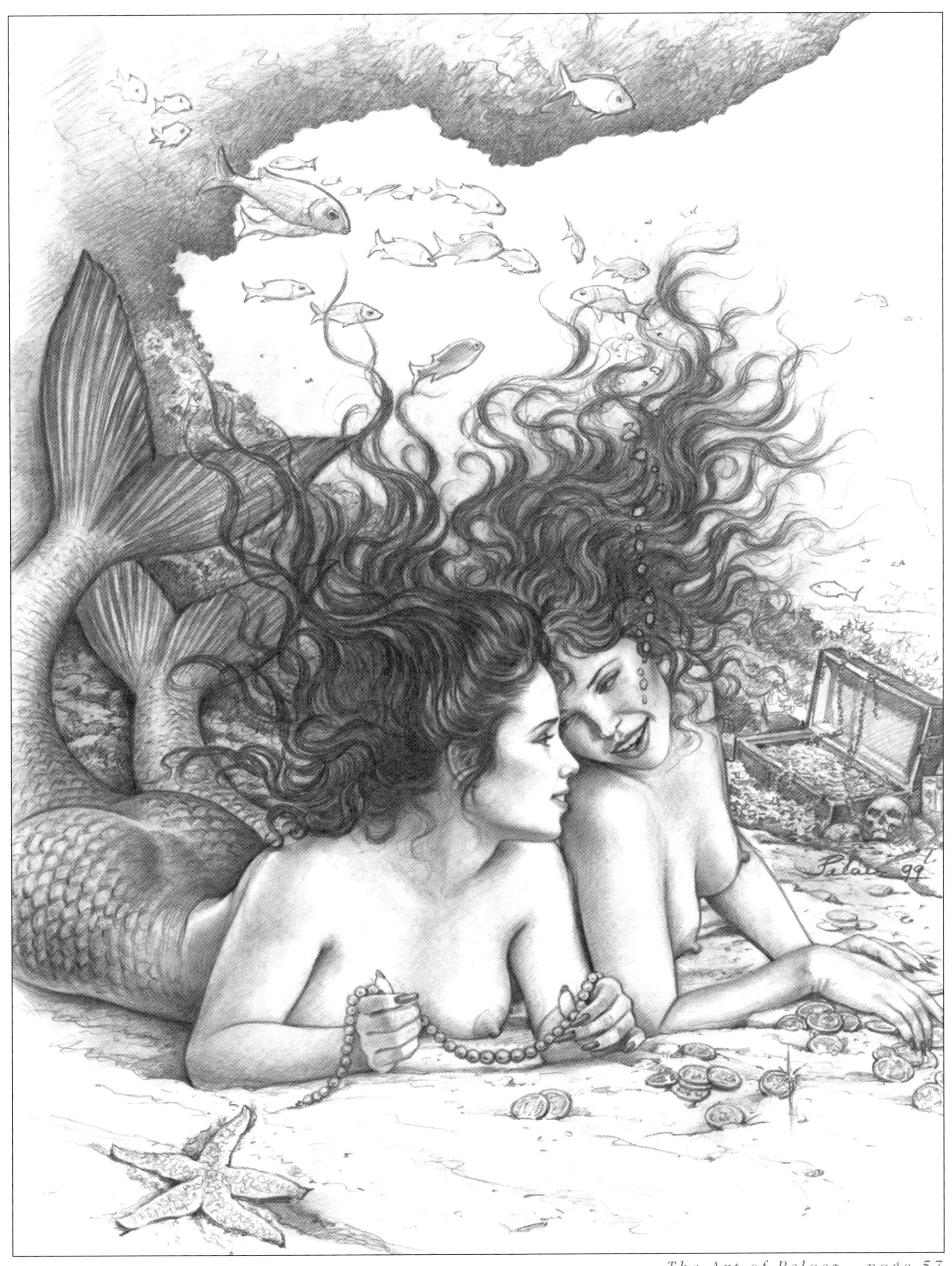
Pelaez 99

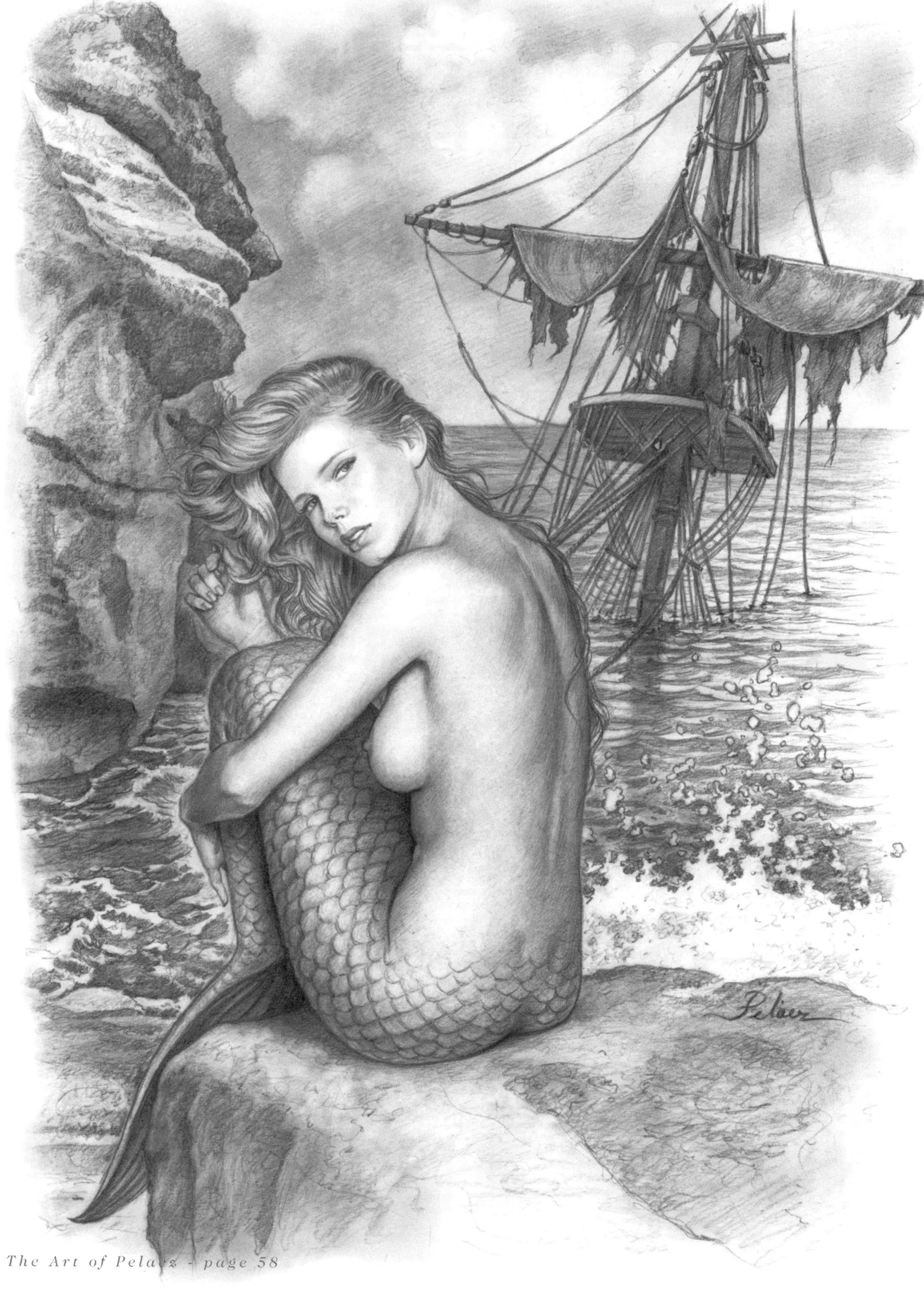
Pelaez

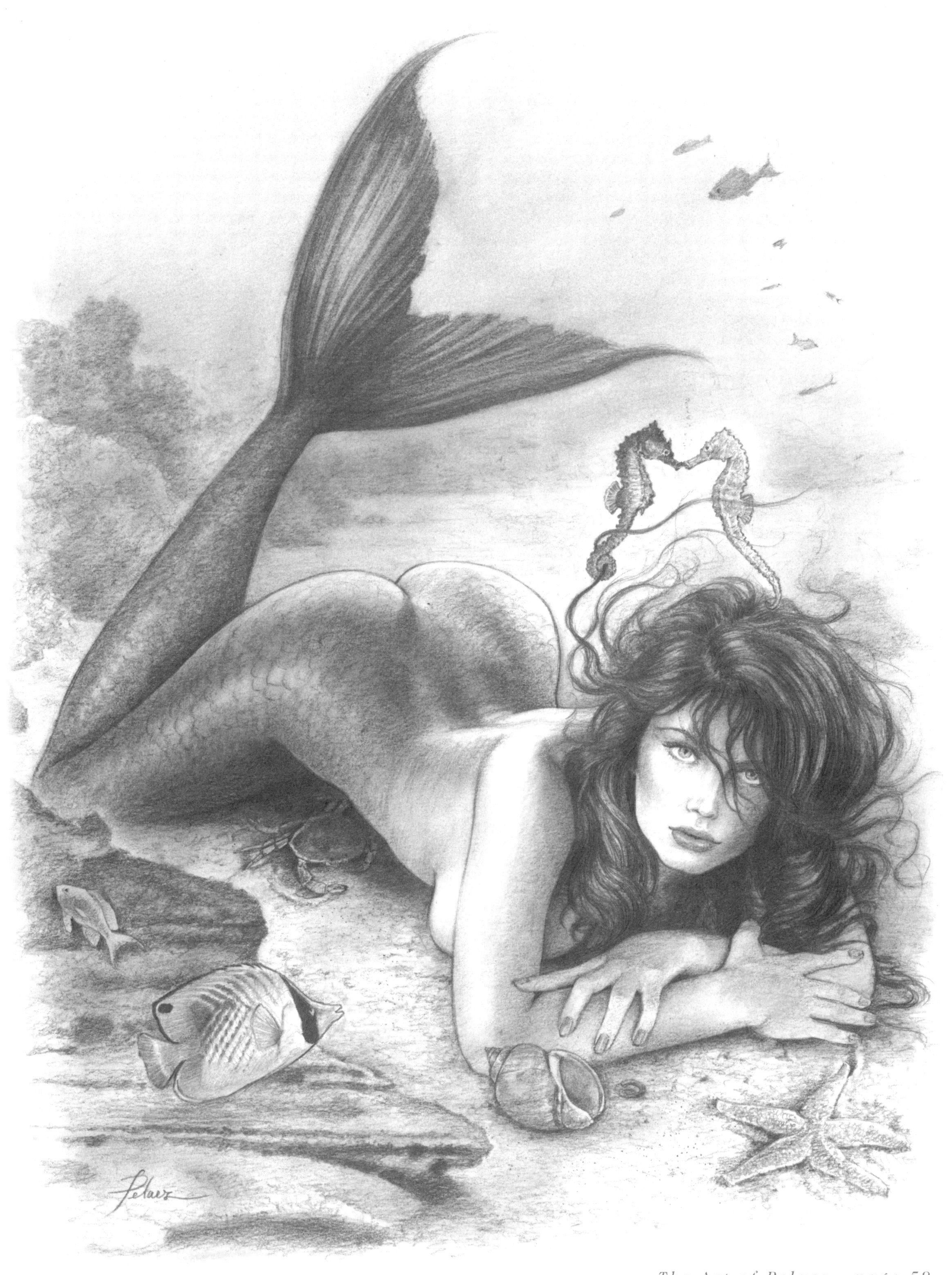
Pelaez

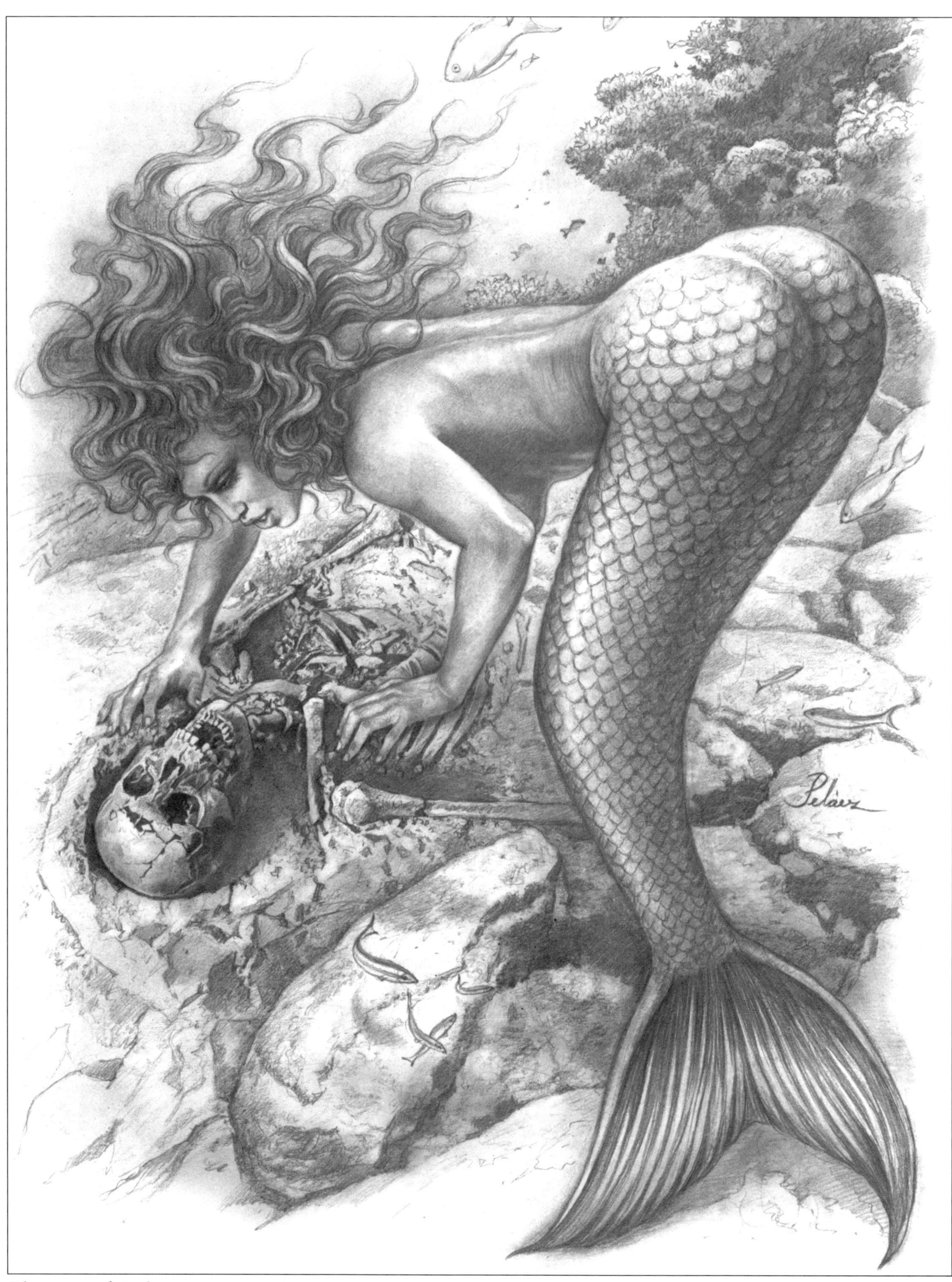
Peláez

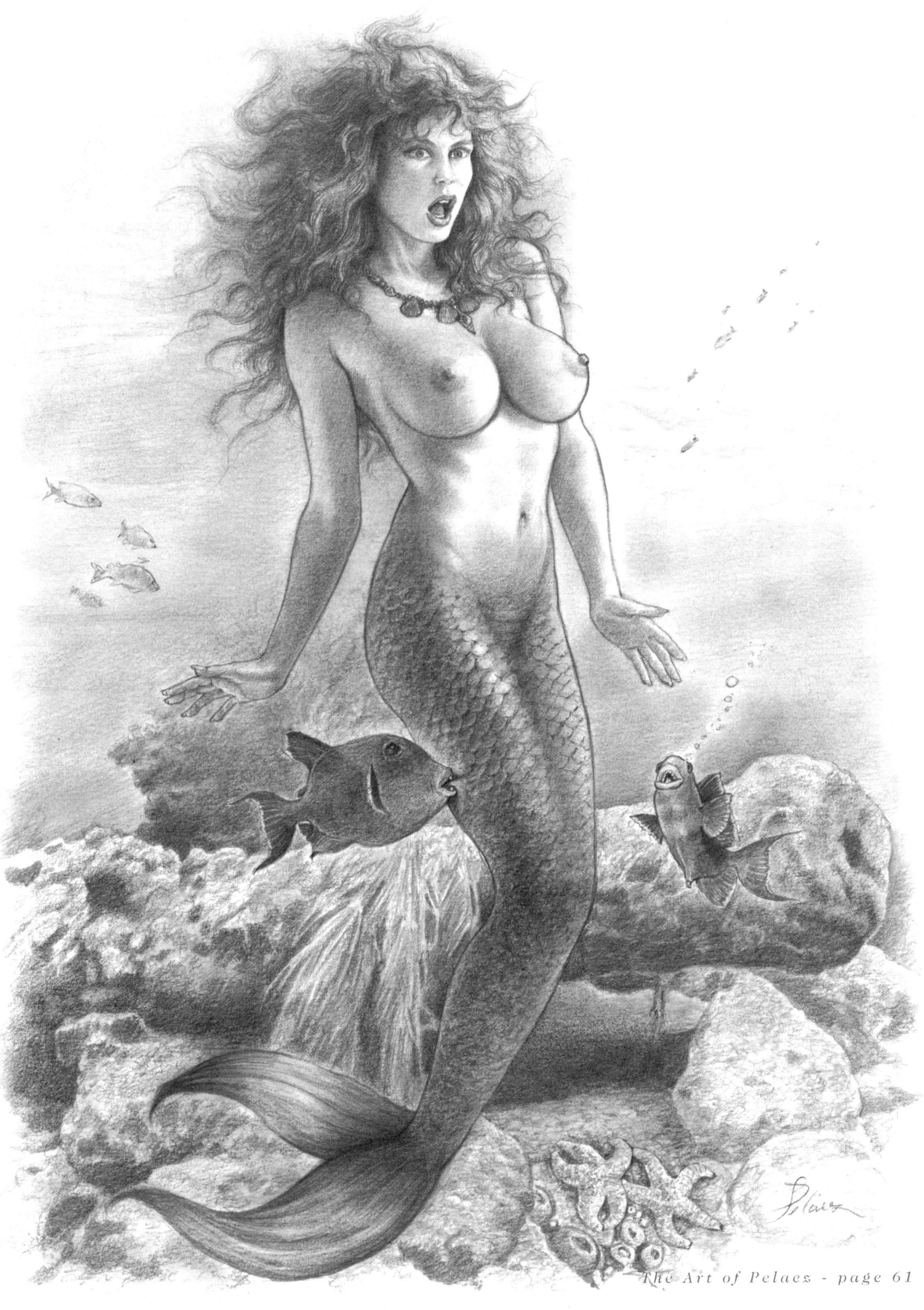

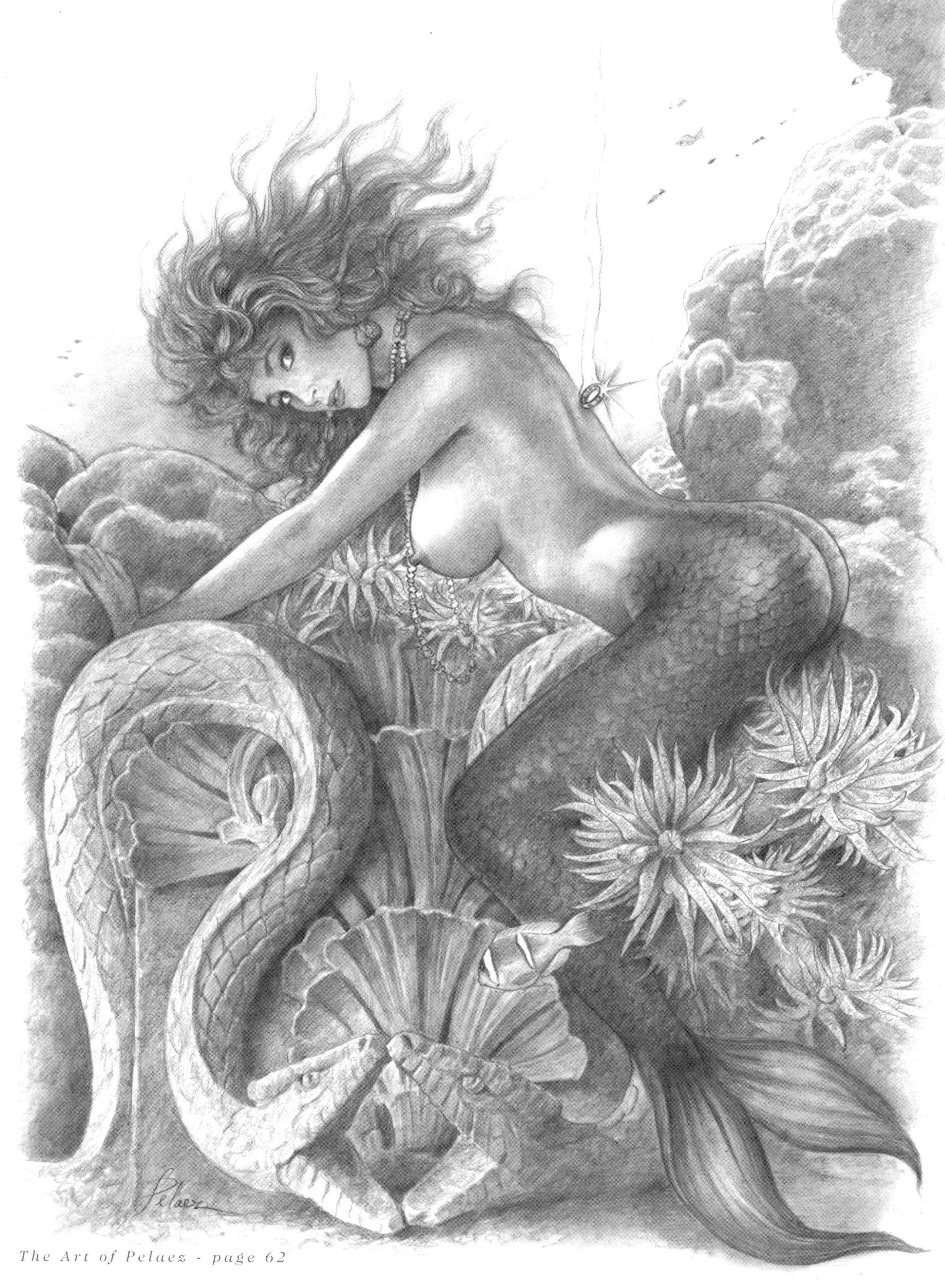
Pelaez

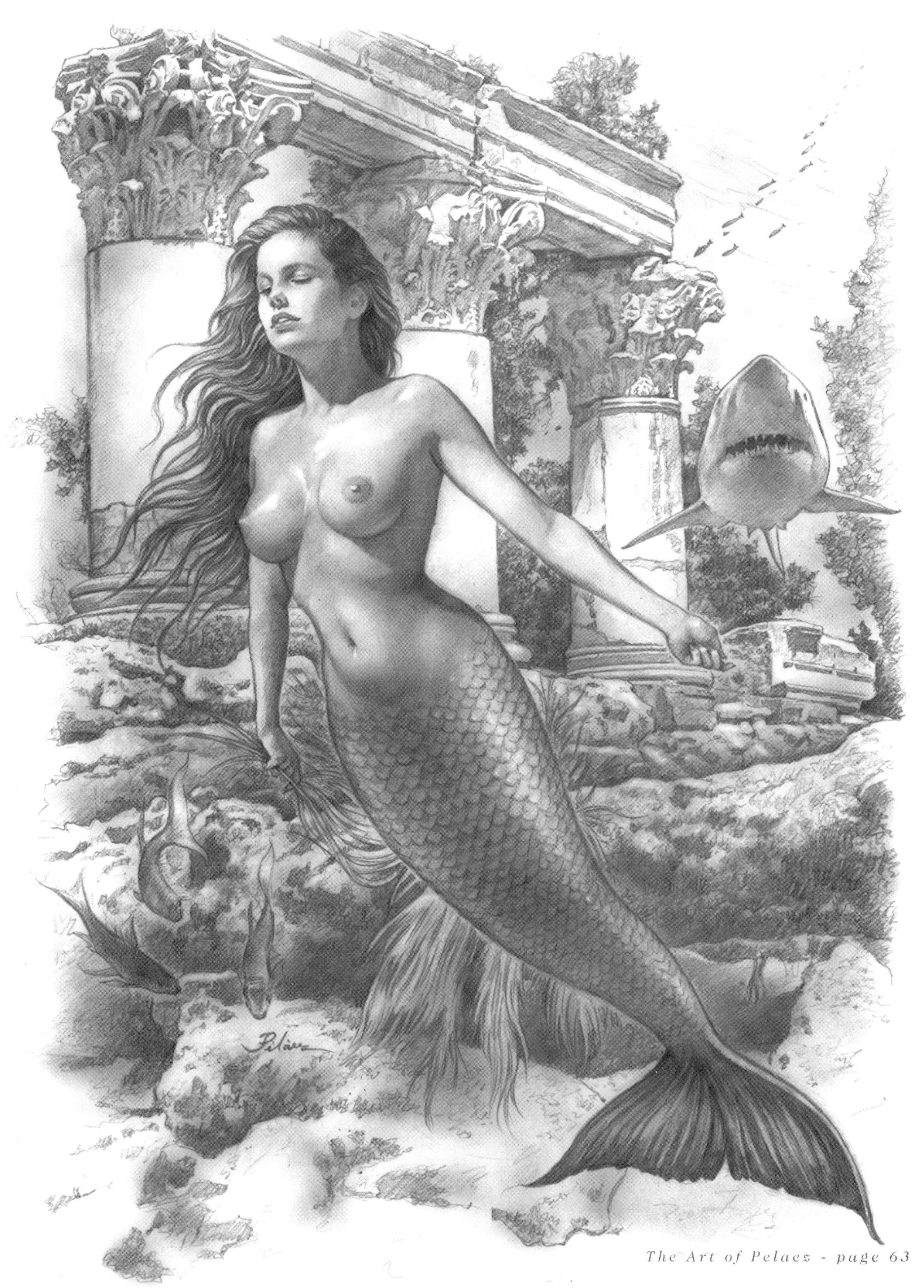
Peláez

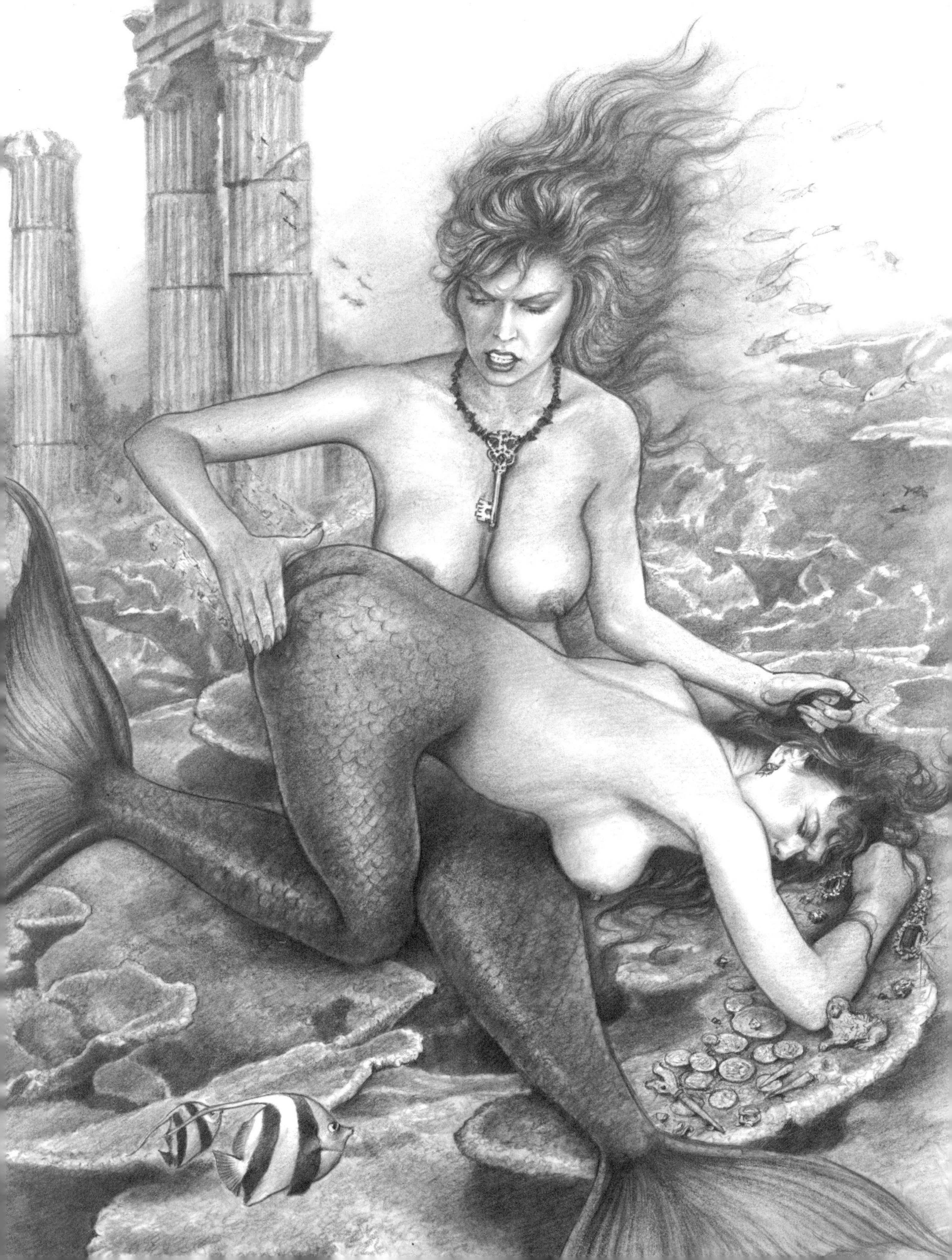